# SpeakEasy's

# Survival Spanish for Construction

*by*
Myelita Melton, MA

SpeakEasy Communications, Inc.

Survival Spanish for Construction

Author: Myelita A. Melton
Cover illustration: Ellen Wass Beckerman
Published by SpeakEasy Communications, Incorporated
116 Sea Trail Drive
Mooresville, NC 28117-8493
USA

ISBN    0-9786998-2-3

Survival Spanish for Construction, SpeakEasy Spanish, SpeakEasy's Survival Spanish, SpeakEasy's Survival Spanish for Construction, and SpeakEasySpanish.com are either trademarks or registered trademarks of SpeakEasy Communications, Incorporated in the United States and/or other countries.

The content of this book is furnished for informational use only, is subject to change without notice, and should not be construed as a commitment by SpeakEasy Communications, Incorporated. SpeakEasy Communications, Incorporated assumes no responsibility or liability for any errors, omissions, or inaccuracies that may appear in the informational content contained in this guide.

# Foreword

I started learning Spanish at seventeen, and it's one of the best decisions I've ever made, especially since it happened by accident. Now, I don't think it was a coincidence. In my senior year of high school I decided to take Spanish instead of Physics. The sciences were never my thing. On the first day of class, I was hooked. The sound of Spanish spoke to my heart, and I knew I had made the right decision. For the next year I begged my parents to let me take my savings and go to Mexico to study. They thought it was a crazy phase I was going through and it would pass eventually. It didn't. Three days after high school graduation I flew to Mexico. ¡Muchas gracias, Mom and Dad! Since high school, Spanish has always been a part of my life and it always will be. I'm glad that you are making Spanish a part of your life too.

Spanish hasn't always come easily to me. There have been plenty of times when I couldn't remember the right word— or any word for that matter. I've also made my share of mistakes, and I'm sure I always will. No matter what, I can say that knowing Spanish has rewarded me richly. It's brought me great friends I would never have had and it's taken me places I would have never been brave enough to go. But best of all, it's given me a greater understanding of Latinos, the most fascinating people on our planet! So, this book is dedicated to you, one of the millions of Americans who want to reach out and make connections with neighbors, friends, colleagues, and customers who speak Spanish. I've loaded it with what I consider to be the essential things that construction professionals should know about one of the most beautiful and expressive languages in the world. ¡Buena suerte, amigos!

Lastly, I'd like to thank to my staff of instructors, proofreaders, artists and editors who catch my mistakes and continue to give me courage. Their time and talents are a constant blessing! Muchas gracias to Ellen Wass Beckerman, Elizabeth Stulz, Candice Tucker, Dr. Leslie Ahmadí, Dr. George Thatcher, Lisa Parker, and Alan Pickelsimer.

# Table of Contents
Survival Spanish for Construction

# Using This Material

Welcome to ***SpeakEasy's Survival Spanish for Construction***. This material is for adults with little or no previous experience in the Spanish language. Through research and interviews with professionals in your field, we have developed this material to be a practical guide to using Spanish on the job. Where ever possible, we have chosen to use the similarities between English and Spanish to facilitate your success.

Throughout the manual you will find study tips and pronunciation guides that will help you to say the words correctly. In the guides, we have broken down the Spanish words for you by syllables, choosing English words that closely approximate the Spanish sound needed. This makes learning Spanish more accessible because it doesn't seem so foreign. When you see letters that are **BOLD** in the guide, say that part of the word the loudest. The bold capital letters are there to show you where the emphasis falls in that particular word.

At SpeakEasy Communications, we believe that ***communication*** is more important than ***conjugation***, and that what you learn should be practical for what you do. We urge you to set realistic goals and to make practice a regular part of your day. You'll be surprised at the progress you make when you learn the SpeakEasy way!

# LATIN AMERICA

## What's The Proper Term?
## Both!

**Latino/Latina**: Anyone from Latin America who speaks Spanish as his or her native language. (Preferred)

**Hispanic**: Anyone who speaks Spanish as his or her native language and traces family origin to Spain.

**Note**: Don't assume that because a person speaks Spanish that they are Mexican. They could be from anywhere in Latin America

---

**Hispanics in the US come mainly from the following three areas:**

1. **Mexico**
2. **Central & South America**
3. **Cuba & Puerto Rico**

*Central America*

---

**According to US Census:.**

1. There are 45.5 million in the US, who speak Spanish.
2. Hispanics are now the majority minority in America (13%).
3. By 2050 Hispanics will make up 25% of the US population.
4. Georgia & NC have the fastest growing Hispanic populations.
5. Over 17% of the nation's school-aged children are Latino.
6. In 2006 Latino buying power surged to over 700 billion dollars.
7. 47% are limited in English proficiency.

---

**Each year Latinos come to America because of natural disasters such as hurricanes or drought. High unemployment in Latin America is also a factor in immigration.**

# SpeakEasy's Secrets to Learning Spanish

***Congratulations on your decision to learn to speak Spanish!*** This is one of the smartest choices you will ever make considering the increasing diversity in our country. It's definitely a decision you will never regret. You are now among a growing number of America's visionary leaders, who want to build better, stronger relationships with Latin Americans, the fastest growing segment of the American workforce.

Learning Spanish is going to open many doors for you, and it will affect you in ways that you can't even imagine. By learning Spanish, you will be able to work more efficiently and safely in almost every workplace in the nation. In addition, you will also be able to give better customer service by building stronger relationships with new Hispanic customers. And-there's another added benefit. You will raise your communication skills to a whole new level.

As an adult, learning a new language requires a certain mind-set. It takes time, patience, and more than a little stubbornness. Just think about it. You didn't learn English overnight- so you can't expect to know everything about Spanish by studying only a few weeks. Adults learn languages quite differently than children do, but you will still make progress quickly by learning practical words and phrases first.

The secret to learning Spanish is having ***self-confidence and a great sense of humor***. To build self-confidence, you must first realize that the entire learning experience is painless and fun. Naturally, you are going to make mistakes. All of us make mistakes in English! So get ready to laugh, learn, and go on from there.

If you took Spanish or another language in high school or college, you are going to be pleasantly surprised when words and phrases you thought you had forgotten begin to come back to you. That previous experience with other languages is still in your mind. It's just hidden away in a little-used filing cabinet. Soon that cabinet will open up again and that's going to help you learn new words even faster.

But there's another idea you should consider, too. What they told you in the traditional foreign language classroom was not exactly correct. There's no such thing as "*perfect Spanish*," just as there is no "*perfect English*." This leaves the door for good communication wide open!

*Español* is one of the world's most beautiful and expressive languages. Consider these other facts as you begin:

✓ English and Spanish share a common Latin heritage, so literally thousands of words in our two languages are either *similar* or *identical*.
✓ Your ability to communicate is the most important thing, so your grammar and pronunciation don't have to be "*perfect*" for you to be understood.
✓ Some very practical and common expressions in Spanish can be communicated with a few simple words.
✓ As the number of Latinos in the United States increases, so do your opportunities to practice. Trying to say even a phrase or two in Spanish every day will help you learn faster.
✓ Relax! People who enjoy their learning experiences seem to acquire Spanish at a much faster pace than others.
✓ Set realistic goals and establish reasonable practice habits.
✓ When you speak even a little Spanish, you are showing a tremendous respect for Hispanic culture and people.
✓ Even a little Spanish or *poco español* goes a long way!

As you begin the process of learning Spanish, you are going to notice a few important differences. Speaking Spanish might feel and sound a little funny to you at first. Don't worry. This is a completely normal. It's because you are using muscles in your face that English doesn't require. Also, your inner ear is accustomed to hearing you speak English. People tell me it sounds and feels like Daffy Duck is inside your head! Just keep going! With practice and perseverance speaking and understanding Spanish will begin to feel more natural to you.

Many Americans know more Spanish than they realize- and pronounce it perfectly. Look at the list on page four and see how many Spanish words you recognize already. Taking the Spanish sounds you already know and practicing them will enable you to learn new principals of the Spanish language easier and faster. This is a great way to build your confidence.

# The Sounds of Spanish

*No se preocupe.* One of your biggest concerns about acquiring a new language will be speaking well enough so that others can understand you. *Don't worry!* Spanish is close enough to English that making a few mistakes along the way won't hurt your ability to communicate.

Here are the *five* vowel sounds in Spanish. These are the most important sounds in this language. Each vowel is pronounced the way it is written. Spanish vowels are never *silent*. Even if there are two vowels together in a word, both of them will stand up and be heard.

| | | |
|---|---|---|
| A | (ah) | as in mama |
| E | (eh) | as in "hay or the "eh" in set |
| I | (ee) | as in deep |
| O | (oh) | as in open |
| U | (oo) | as in spoon |

Here are other sounds you'll need to remember. Always pronounce them the same way. Spanish is a very consistent language. The sounds the letters make don't shift around as they do in English.

| | *Spanish Letter* | *English Sound* |
|---|---|---|
| C | (before an e or i) | s as in Sam: **cero: SAY**-row |
| G | (before an e or i) | h as in he: **energía:** n-air-**HE**-ah |
| H | | silent: **hacienda**: ah-see-**N**-da |
| J | | h as in hot: **Julio, HOO**-lee-oh |
| LL | | y as in yoyo: **tortilla**, tor- **TEE**-ya |
| Ñ | | ny as in canyon: **español**, es-pan- **NYOL** |
| QU | | k as in kit: **tequila**, tay-**KEY**-la |
| RR | | The "trilled" r sound: **burro**, **BOO**-row |
| V | | v as in Victor: **Victor**, Vic-**TOR** |
| Z | | s as in son: **Gonzales**, gone-**SA**-les |

*The Other Consonants* - The remaining letters in Spanish are very similar to their equivalents in English.

# The Spanish Alphabet
El alphabeto español

| A | ah | J | HO-ta | R | AIR-ray |
|---|---|---|---|---|---|
| B | bay | K | ka | RR | EH-rray |
| C | say | L | L-ay | S | S-ay |
| CH | chay | LL | A-yea | T | tay |
| D | day | M | M-ay | U | oo |
| E | A or EH | N | N-ay | V | vay |
| F | f-ay | Ñ | N-yea | W | DOE-blay-vay |
| G | hay | O | oh | X | 'a-kees |
| H | AH-chay | P | pay | Y | ee-gree-A-gah |
| I | ee | Q | coo | Z | SAY-ta |

# The Spanish Accent

In Spanish you will see two accent marks. Both are very important and do different things. One of the diacritical marks you will notice is called a "tilde." It is only found over the letter "N." But, don't get the Ñ confused with N. The accent mark over Ñ makes it into a different letter entirely. In fact, it's one of four letters in the Spanish alphabet that the English alphabet doesn't have. The Ñ changes the sound of the letter to a combination of "ny." You'll hear the sound that this important letter makes in the English words "canyon" and "onion."

Occasionally you will see another accent mark over a letter in a Spanish word. The accent mark or "slash" mark shows you where to place vocal emphasis. So, when you see an accent mark over a letter in a Spanish word, just say that part of the word louder. For example: José (ho-**SAY**). These accented syllables are indicated in our pronunciation guides with bold, capital letters.

# Pronouncing Spanish Words

The pronunciation of Spanish words follows more regular rules than most other languages. That makes it easier to learn. Here are some tips to remember.

1. Most Spanish words that end with vowels are stressed or emphasized on the ***next to the last*** syllable.
2. Look for an accent mark. If the Spanish word has an accent in it, that's the emphasized syllable.
3. Words that end in consonants are stressed on the ***final*** syllable.

# Spanish Punctuation Marks

You will see two different punctuation marks in Spanish. First there's the upside down question mark (¿). You will see it at the beginning of all questions. It's there to simply let you know that what follows is a question and you will need to give your voice an upward inflection. It's the same inflection we use in English. Then, there's the upside down exclamation mark (¡). It's there to let you know that what follows should be vocally emphasized.

# Spanglish

When the US-Mexican War ended in 1848, Mexico ceded much of the Southwest to the United States. This transformed Spanish-speaking Mexicans into Americans overnight! Just imagine waking up one morning to find out you're a citizen of another country! This merging of cultures caused a synthesis of languages. A new language was born that mixes the best of both worlds. It's called ***Spanglish***. People who use Spanglish span generations and nationalities. It's heard in music, seen in print, and used in conversations all through the Americas. Immigrants learning

English may turn to Spanglish out of necessity and bilingual speakers use it because it's convenient. Even thought it's still frowned upon in most traditional language classes, it really is a great tool. Here are some of our *favoritos*.

| Truck/Trocka | Lunch/Lonche | No parking/No parque |
|---|---|---|
| Yard/Yarda | Break/Breaka | Cell Phone/El cel |

Some Spanglish words are spelled and pronounced exactly as they are in English, while others take on a more Spanish spelling. Do an on-line search to learn more about Spanglish. You'll even find Spanglish dictionaries!

| Aplicación | Baquear |
|---|---|
| Bar | Internet |
| Biles | Blinquear |
| Break time | Party |
| Culer | CD |
| Dishwasher | Rock-n-roll |
| Email | Record |
| Eventualmente | Flonguear |
| Ganga | Insulación |
| Jandimán | Liqueur |
| Pantijós | Rentar |
| Rufero | Sortear |
| Rufo | Mol |
| Stress | Six-pack |
| Supermarket | Pizza |

# More Amigos Similares y Familiares

Using what you've learned about the sounds of Spanish, practice the words below. Many will be words you already know or have heard before, while others will be completely new to you. There are some Spanglish words in the list too. Begin by examining each word. Some will be useful to you at work. Pronounce each one carefully. After you've pronounced each word, go back through them again marking the ones you can use on the job. Practice these words often to help you remember the basic sounds of *español*.

## Easy Amigos

| | | |
|---|---|---|
| Accidente | Arnés | Áttico |
| Banco | Baño | Bistec |
| Brocha | Cacerola | Calidad |
| Carpeta | Carro | Cliente |
| Compañía | Construcción | Contaminación |
| Corredor | Defecto | Doctor |
| Dormitorio | Electricidad | Empleo |
| Escalera | Especial | Estudio |
| Extensión | Familia | Fiesta |
| Fluorescente | Fotografía | Función |
| Galón | Garaje | Gasolina |
| Hospital | Identificación | Inglés |
| Instrucción | Jalapeño | Máquina |
| Metal | Motor | Música |
| No parque | Objectivo | Oficina |
| Operar | Oportunidad | Patio |
| Plataforma | Problema | Producción |
| Pronto | Rápido | Refrigerador |
| Segundo | Selección | Servicio |
| Supervisor | Talento | Teléfono |
| Temperatura | Vacación | Vapor |
| Velocidad | Ventilador | Vestíbulo |

# Muchos Ways to Practicar

The more you listen to and use your *español* the easier it will be to learn it. There are lots of great ways to practice that won't cost your any money. Try these practice techniques for improving your skills:

- ✓ Next time you're at a Mexican restaurant, order your food in *español*.
- ✓ Start slowly. Practice one sound each week.
- ✓ Read Spanish language newspapers. They are usually free and easily available.
- ✓ Listen to Spanish language radio stations.
- ✓ Watch Spanish language television via satellite.
- ✓ Rent Spanish language videos, especially cartoons.
- ✓ Buy Spanish tapes and listen to them in the car while you commute.
- ✓ And speaking of tapes, there is such a variety of Latin *música* available, something will be right for you. Listening to music is a great way to train your ears to Spanish and have fun doing it. Personally, I like anything by Carlos Santana or the Salsa music of Marc Anthony. What do you like?
- ✓ Visit Internet sites like *www.about.com* or *www.studyspanish.com*, where you can find all kinds of information about the Spanish language. They have a wonderful newsletter that comes to you free via e-mail. Most search engines, like Yahoo, have some sort of Spanish section.
- ✓ Next time you listen to a baseball game, keep track of all the Hispanic names you hear.
- ✓ Practice your Spanish every time the opportunity presents itself. This is the only way to get over your nervousness.
- ✓ Try to learn with a friend at work and practice together.

*What practice habits work for you?*
*Share them with us at:*
*info@speakeasyspanish.com*

# SpeakEasy's Tips and Techniques for Comunicación

**Remember**, when you're trying to communicate with a person who is "limited in English proficiency," *patience is a virtue*! Here are some easy things you can do to make the conversation easier for both of you. For more information on LEP visit this web site: www.lep.gov

✓ Speak slowly and distinctly.

✓ Do not use slang expressions or colorful terms.

✓ Get straight to the point! Unnecessary words cloud your meaning.

✓ Speak in a normal tone. Speaking *loudly* doesn't help anyone understand you any better!

✓ Look for cues to meaning in body language and facial expressions. Use gestures of your own to get your point across.

✓ You may not receive good eye contact.

✓ Latinos tend to stand closer to each other than North Americans do when they talk to each other, so your personal space could feel crowded. Stand your ground!

✓ Feel free to use gestures and body language of your own to communicate.

✓ Because of the way languages are learned, it is likely that the person you are talking to understands more of what you are saying, than he is able to verbalize. *So, be careful what you say!* No matter what the language, we always understand the bad words first!

## Tips & Tidbits
Throughout your book look for the light bulb you see above. This section will give you helpful hints and important cultural information.

# Managing in a Multicultural Environment

Effective management and training in a multicultural environment requires at least a basic knowledge of your employee's culture and traditions. Familiarity with both is essential because each has a bearing on a person's every day behavior on and off the job. Where you come from doesn't matter where heritage is concerned. Everyone feels very strongly about it because it's a unique part of our background. Our cultural identity helps us feel like we are "part" of the society around us. It keeps us from feeling isolated and sometimes it helps us know how to react. As Americans, we know it's appropriate to stand when we hear *The Star Spangled Banner* because it's part of our culture. Traditions involving family, religion, education, and nationalism play a large role in any employee's attitude towards professional life. Personal appearance, ethics, and etiquette are also factors to be considered. Whether we realize it or not, culture and tradition are powerful principles we carry with us daily. It's almost like carrying a cell phone. We take it for granted that our phone is in our pocket, but we don't realize it until it rings. Culture is very much like that. It's always with you even though you are unaware of it. Then you hear or see something that rings your cultural bell. That's when culture and tradition can make even the most level-headed person make very emotional decisions.

Even though it's hard to make broad generalizations about culture, many studies have been conducted over the years on its importance to Latin Americans. There are certain basic principles about Latin American culture and tradition that make good survival skills for American employers. This section outlines some of the most ***importante***.

**La Familia:** The first cultural principle employers should examine carefully is the importance of family. An intense love of family is a strong feature in Latinos. Nuclear families are the foundation of Hispanic society. To most, the family and its needs are more important than work. Working is often seen as a "necessary evil" done for the purpose of earning enough money to satisfy the needs of the family with some left over for the really important things in life: enjoying the company of family and friends. Work should be enjoyed during daylight hours. That leaves quality time in the evening to spend with family. Most Latin Americans prefer not to take the job home because it intrudes on family life. For most employers, this is hard to understand and accept. This is specially true when an employer wants to promote a Latino employee and finds that they prefer to remain in a position that will give them time with family in spite of the pay increase added responsibility brings. Many say that Americans live to work and work to live. Most managers put in hours of overtime and go to work on weekends. For managers in American companies, work even intrudes on vacation time since many of us take business calls when we are off and take time daily to check our email. Latinos prefer to separate their family lives from their business lives and don't want work to be intrusive into what is really important—*la familia*.

**La Structura:** The structure of typical Latin American families is also different from most American families. Almost always the father is the undisputed head of the household. He makes all major family decisions. In US most family decisions are shared between husbands and wives.

Next let's consider *los niños*. Children in Latino families are cherished, protected and loved. A typical weekend is spent enjoying time together, preparing meals, visiting friends, or extended family. Children are more heavily influenced by their parents and extended family members than by those outside the family. In some cases American kids are more profoundly influenced by their peers or the media than they are by their parents. American children also tend to be more independent at a younger age. We want to raise our children to "stand on their own two feet," whereas many Hispanic parents  concentrate on raising their children to be strong members of their extended families. The family is more important than the individual.

As managers we must also take into consideration the fact that many Hispanic employees have left members of their families behind to take jobs in the United States. This is a sad and complicated fact that occurs for a variety of reasons. Average wages in Latin America are often no more than pennies per hour, not nearly enough to provide basic necessities. In many countries infrastructure is woefully inadequate, and poverty is overwhelming. Often electricity and clean water in the home is still a luxury. Children leave school to go to work so they can help their families. According to the US Census in 2000, 27% of Hispanics over the age of twenty-five had no more than a ninth grade education. Low wages and poverty lead to poor healthcare, lack of good nutrition and a sense of desperation that we can't understand. ***Personal sacrifice is the rule, not the exception.*** The estrangement and isolation that comes with being separated from parents, wives and children can be devastating. This causes severe depression, isolation and even substance abuse. Each of these becomes high risk factors for on the job accidents.

**La Religión:** Religion and spirituality are also deeply rooted in Latin American culture. Almost 90% Latin Americans are Roman Catholic and most observe basic religious traditions such as baptisms, first communion, marriages and funerals, even though they might not attend church on a regular basis. Throughout Latin America religious practices play a more visible role in the workplace than they do in the US. Anywhere south of the US border it isn't uncommon to see a religious image displayed in a prominent place at work. A priest might also be called in to bless a new building or business endeavor. Many Hispanic managers feel these practices make a valuable contribution to overall worker morale.

An unusual feature of Latin American spirituality is an indefinable fatalism or ***fatalismo*** which is pervasive in the culture. Many Latinos have the underlying sense that their lives are controlled by fate; consequently, whatever success or tragedy befalls them is no result of their own actions. There's no point in being competitive because whatever happens will happen. ***Qué será será.*** This is almost opposite of the American belief that our success or lack of it depends solely on the choices we make and the hard work we put into it.

**Nacionalismo:** Nationalism is deeply ingrained in Hispanics. This is a fact that most Americans don't realize fully. When we see a person speaking Spanish, we automatically assume that the person is Mexican. Often that just isn't true. Spanish is spoken over a wide area that includes eighteen very different countries. If the person comes from a country other than Mexico, this assumption is extremely offensive. All of us are deeply proud of our roots. Latin Americans have deep attachments to their homelands and the unique culture that comes with that. Because you speak English, would you like to be mistaken for a Canadian instead of an American? Probably not! It's savvy management for employers to know which countries their employees come from. Getting to know individual employees is a basic feature in successful Latin American management strategies. The boss becomes personally acquainted with each employee and knows a bit about his family. This is called *personalizmo*, and it's very important to workplace attitudes. When *el jefe* or *el supervisor* recognizes an individual employee, he feels more respected and valued. That increases his loyalty to the company and to its leadership.

Many Americans don't realize how truly different each Latin American country is. People from Venezuela don't enjoy the same taste in foods as those from Peru or Bolivia. Everyone doesn't like *jalapeños* and spicy dishes. There's also a wide variety in music and even fashion.

**Los Acentos:** As you begin to study Spanish, it's also important for you to realize that how *español* is spoken in each country is different too. Accents and some vocabulary can shift from place to place. That shouldn't be surprising to Americans since our accents change from region to region.

Obviously, people who live in Atlanta speak English differently from those who live in Brooklyn. The same can be said of Spanish. Regional accents are common, but it's still *español.* The differences between Latin American lifestyles and language make Hispanic heritage extremely rich. The culture is as colorful and complicated as any on earth. It is the Spanish language and a few core principles that bind Latinos into a cohesive group. Understanding and appreciating the *diversidad* in Latin America is the key to truly understanding its culture.

**La Etiqueta:** Basic etiquette and social skills are also valued by Latin Americans. Good manners are a sign of solid upbringing. Training begins at the home and continues in school. Great emphasis is attached to shaking hands and greeting the staff each morning in the workplace. Not only is this sort of etiquette valued in face to face interactions, it's also a part of good telephone etiquette. In a Latin American's eyes it's rude to "cut to the chase" on the telephone and immediately begin to discuss business without first asking how the person is that you are talking to. Next, to be truly polite you should ask how the family is doing. Etiquette is so important on the job many think *por favor* and *gracias* are the two most important phrases in the Spanish language. These are definitely words that will help you get the job done.

Etiquette is also an extremely important feature in the Spanish language. *Español* is very specific in the vocabulary used to denote personal relationships. Specificity in usage is one feature that makes Spanish such a powerful language. Little is left to interpretation because of added details in vocabulary and description. Spanish is so specific that there are two words in it for "you." First there is *Usted*. It is used when you are speaking with business acquaintances, strangers and most adults. *Usted* inherently shows politeness and respect to others. The word "*tú*" is reserved for close personal friends and members of the family. While Americans jump to informality by using first names almost immediately, this can be interpreted as rudeness in Latin American society. That's because a relationship has not yet been built. In Spanish great emphasis is placed on the use of courtesy titles such as *Señor*, *Señora* or *Señorita*. In Latin America there is a real difference between a *friend* and an *acquaintance*; consequently, in most business situations it is better to address an employee *Señor* or *Señora* followed by his or her last name instead of using a first name only—especially at first. This shows respect for the individual and leads to good morale in the workplace.

**La Lealtad:** Loyalty and quality of work are other hallmarks of Hispanic employees. Historically, Latin American workers have demonstrated exceptional loyalty to *el jefe* or the boss. *Personalismo* or the "cult of personality" still can play a significant role in staff loyalty. In the past that was often a more important factor than company loyalty which is stressed in American companies. At one time *el jefe* was a very paternalistic sort of figure. He was so important in the lives of Hispanic workers they would often ask his advice even on personal problems. But in Latin American firms this has created some inherent communication problems. Employees only tell *el jefe* what he *wants* to hear and not what he *needs* to hear. American employees "tell it like it is" and "let the chips fall where they may" with no regard for what management wants to hear. Promoting open communication between management and staff is an important factor in integrating a multicultural workforce. As business practices change, the relationship between employees and management change. Now personnel policies and pay greatly influence the Hispanic workforce. A friendly working atmosphere where policies are discussed with employees is also essential. This in turn decreases employee turnover and promotes a positive, safe working environment where workers feel free to discuss even the most sensitive issues.

**El tiempo:** Time and time management are also concepts where Latin Americans and Americans differ greatly. The Hispanic attitude toward time is often called the "*mañana*" or tomorrow complex. It's taken to mean what ever you need done will not be done today—and it doesn't necessarily mean that it will be done tomorrow either. The day after tomorrow will be just as good! In business this goes back to the premise that you will be told what you want to hear. If you want to hear that your shipment or job will be done tomorrow, that's what you will be told. No one wants to disappoint you or hurt your feelings. You are told what will make you happy. When the job isn't completed as you were told, a good explanation will be given to you that saves face for everyone. That's very important. A time commitment is always a good objective, but it isn't binding. For Americans, who always strive to be on time, love punctuality and believe that everything should run according to schedule, this laid-back style can be interpreted as laziness when in actuality it isn't. This is hard to understand in a workplace where "time is money" and there isn't a second to waste.

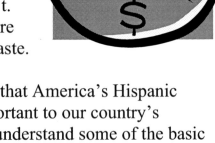

**Strategies for Success:** There's no doubt that America's Hispanic workforce is going to become even more important to our country's economic growth and success. Now that you understand some of the basic attitudes your Hispanic workforce has, it's time to plot a course for your success in a multicultural environment.

1. *Work aggressively to overcome the language barrier*. Obviously, this means learning to speak some Spanish. You don't have to be fluent to be successful. Employers who have a basic knowledge of Spanish gain the respect of employees for making the attempt. You re also setting a great example which will encourage your Spanish-speaking employees to learn English. It's also important to remember that employers who learn Spanish will avoid the problem of having a Spanish-speaking employee control all the communication that takes

place between management and staff. Even though it is important to encourage and to promote bilingual employees, you want to be able to understand and participate in any discussion of your firm's employment practices and policies.

2. ***Make every effort to learn about the culture of your employees.*** Learning about culture enables employers to better understand their employees as people. This will help you build the relationships that Latinos value so much. In addition, you will also understand the supervisory techniques that are acceptable and unacceptable to employees from another culture. Use several different strategies to develop cultural understanding. First, become familiar with the employees' culture by asking them to describe life back home. Next, they read about the culture of your employees and contrast it with the American culture. There are many great books available that will help you. See the suggested reading list at the back of this book for more information. The more you understand about your employee's culture and heritage the more you will be able to help them develop an appreciation for American culture. This will help your workforce integrate and develop respect for each other.

3. ***Develop an open culture in your workplace that accepts and appreciates the differences individual employees bring to your organization.*** Help all of your employees recognize and appreciate the differences between cultures. One of the realities of integrating people of different races and cultures is that occasionally racism or prejudice emerges. This creates tension and disrespect within the workgroup. Effective managers address these derisive issues quickly and directly by insisting that all employees be treated with respect and dignity regardless of race or cultural background. Effective managers also create opportunities for supervisors and employees to learn about the culture of their Hispanic employees and to appreciate it. Successful employers also take a proactive role in helping Hispanic employees to adjust to the work environment and making them comfortable with their new job. The extra time you take to make this effort will be well worth it.

4. ***Establish employment policies carefully and communicate them so all employees understand your expectations for appropriate conduct on the job.*** Employment policies must be uniformly enforced with all employees. To be effective, set goals for all employees at the beginning of the employment relationship. Work hour requirements, performance requirements, and conduct are all-important issues to cover.

5. ***As required by law, make every effort to hire employees who have legally entered the country.*** Employers have a legal responsibility to check for proper identification of all employees. Fill out an I-9 form on each employee you hire and keep it on file. Make sure you fully understand the serious consequences you risk by hiring undocumented employees.

6. ***Acknowledge your employees' strong family ties and desire to return home periodically.*** Make every effort to develop staffing that is flexible enough to allow employees to return home for a period of time to visit their families and then return to the job. Many employees earn money to support families at home and often send most of their earnings back to their family at home. Statistically, this can be as much as 85% of their total wages. Recognizing the importance of family ties and providing time off without penalties when ever possible will create a stronger, more loyal and motivated Hispanic workforce. Insist on open communication by asking for several weeks notice before family leave is taken so you can ensure that efficient operation continues in your organization. This will help you see the absence ahead of time so you can plan for it. For many first generation employees working is a means to spending more time with family.

# Beginning Words & Phrases

Well, let's get started! In no time you will start gaining confidence. Latinos will be delighted that you are trying to speak *español*. Even if you can't remember a whole phrase, use the words you know. Thank you *gracias* and please *por favor* go a long way toward establishing a rapport.

How many of these common words and phrases do you know?

| English | Español | Guide |
|---------|---------|-------|
| Hi! | ¡Hola! | **OH**-la |
| How are you? | ¿Cómo está? | **KO**-mo ace-**TA** |
| Fine | Muy bien. | mooy b-**N** |
| So so | Así así | ah-**SEE** ah-**SEE** |
| Bad | Mal | mal |
| Good morning | Buenos días | boo-**WAY**-nos **DEE**-ahs |
| Good afternoon | Buenas tardes | boo-**WAY**-nas **TAR**-days |
| Good night | Buenas noches. | boo-**WAY**-nas **NO**-chase |
| Sir or Mister | Señor | sen-**YOUR** |
| Mrs. or Ma'am | Señora | sen-**YOUR**-ah |
| Miss | Señorita | sen-your-**REE**-ta |
| What's your name? | ¿Cómo se llama? | **KO**-mo say **YA**-ma |
| My name is ___. | Me llamo ___. | may **YA**-mo |
| Nice to meet you. | ¡Mucho gusto! | **MOO**-cho **GOO**-stow |
| Thank you. | Gracias. | **GRA**-see-ahs |
| Please! | ¡Por favor! | pour-fa-**VOR** |
| You're welcome. The pleasure is mine. | De nada. El gusto es mío. | day **NA** da el **GOO**-stow es **ME**-oh |
| I'm sorry. | Lo siento. | low-see-**N**-toe |
| Excuse me. | ¡Perdón! | pear-**DON** |
| Bless you! | ¡Salud! | sah-**LEWD** |
| We'll see you! | ¡Hasta la vista! | **AH**-sta la **V**-sta |
| Good-bye | Adiós | ah-dee-**OS** |

# Spanish Sounds Rápido – What Do I Do Now?

*Be honest!* One of the reasons you are hesitant to speak Spanish is that it sounds so fast! Naturally, you're afraid you won't understand. Here are some phrases that will help you. Make learning them a priority. *¿Comprende, amigo?*

| English | Español | Guide |
|---|---|---|
| I don't understand. | No comprendo. | no com-**PREN**-doe |
| Do you understand | ¿Comprende? | com-**PREN**-day |
| I speak a little Spanish. | Hablo poco español. | **AH**-blow **POE**-co es-pan-**NYOL** |
| Do you speak English? | ¿Habla inglés? | **AH**-bla eng-**LACE** |
| Repeat, please. | Repita, por favor. | ray-**PETE**-ah pour fa-**VOR** |
| I'm studying Spanish. | Estudio español. | es-**TOO**-dee-oh es-pan-**NYOL** |
| Write it, please | Escribe, por favor | es-**SCRE**-bay pour fa-**VOR** |
| Speak more slowly, please. | Habla más despacio, por favor. | **AH**-bla mas des-**PA**-see-oh pour fa-**VOR** |
| Thanks for your patience. | Gracias por su paciencia. | **GRA**-see-ahs pour sue pa-see-**N**-see-ah |
| How do you say it in Spanish? | ¿Como se dice en español? | **CO**-mo say **DEE**-say n ace-pan-**NYOL** |
| Where are you from? | ¿De dónde es? | day **DON**-day ace |
| May I help you? | ¿Puedo servirle? | pooh-**A**-doe seer-**VEER**-lay |

*The key here is <u>not</u> to pánico.*

Your Spanish-speaking employee or friend is having just as much trouble understanding you, as you are having understanding them! Hang in there! Between the two of you, *comunicación* will begin to take place.

# SpeakEasy's Conversaciones

## Practice Conversation I

| | |
|---|---|
| **USTED**: | Good morning, Sir. |
| **SR. GARCÍA** | Good morning. How are you? |
| **USTED** | Fine, thanks. How are you? |
| **SR. GARCÍA** | OK, thanks. |

## Practice Conversation II

**USTED**   May I help you? My name is _____.
I speak a little Spanish. What's your name?

¡Hola!

**SRA. GARCÍA:**   My name is Carla García Hernandez. I speak a little English.

**USTED**   Nice to meet you.

**SRA. GARCÍA**   Yes, nice to meet you.

## Can you say the following?

✓ Good morning or hi

✓ My name is _____.

✓ I speak a little Spanish.

✓ Do you speak English?

✓ Slower, please. Thank you.

# ¿Cuál Es Su Nombre Completo?

What Is Your Complete Name?

# Hispanic Names Have Four Parts

| First Name | Middle Name | Father's Surname | Mother's Surname |
|---|---|---|---|
| Primer Nombre | Segundo Nombre | Apellido Paterno | Apellido Materno |
| Carlos | Jesús | Santana | Rodríguez |
| José | Pedro | Cuervo | Álvarez |
| Poncho | Luis | Villa | García |
| Carmen | Elena | Miranda | Rivera |

**Start with**: Señor, Señora, or Señorita

## Use Both Names Or Only The Father's Last Name

Sr. Santana                     Sr. Cuervo
Sr. Villa                           Sra. Miranda

## When A Woman Marries

She Keeps Her Father's Apellido Paterno
She Drops Her Apellido Materno
Last Is Her Husband's Apellido Paterno
Ask for her "Apellido Paterno de Esposo"

## Children Have The Apellido Paterno of Both Father and Mother

*If Carlos Santana married Carmen Miranda,
what is the Nombre Completo of the bebé*

**José Carlos ????  ?????**

*Answer: José Carlos Santana Miranda*

# Spanish Nouns

Can words *really* have a gender?

¡Sí! Spanish belongs to the "romance" language family. It doesn't have anything to do with love, but it has a lot to do with the Romans. In ancient times people had the same trouble learning languages that they do today—except that there were no cassette tapes, CDs, PDAs or very many foreign language teachers. In those days, there weren't many schools for that matter! Consequently, most folks were on their own when it came to learning another language.

To help the difficult process along, words were placed into categories based on how they sounded. This organized the material and made it easier to learn. Old-world languages had many different categories and because the categories were often called "masculine," "feminine," or even "neuter," people began talking about words in terms of their gender. Even though the word "gender" is misleading, the tendency to group words by sound helped people learn new languages more quickly.

Because Spanish evolved from Latin, it has maintained two category divisions for thousands of years. The categories are called masculine and feminine. Even though Spanish can and will evolve, the concept of categories in español is not likely to change.

Here are the most important points to remember about nouns and their categories:

**NOUN**

**A person, place or thing**

1. Usually, the words are grouped by how they sound, not by what they mean. There will always be a few exceptions!

2. Languages are a lot like the people who use them: They don't always follow the rules!

3. If the Spanish noun is referring to a person, the letter will often indicate the sex of that individual. For example: a doctor, who is a man is a "doctor," while a woman, who is a doctor is a "doctora."

4. Words in the "masculine" category usually end with the letter "O".

5. Words in the "feminine" category usually end with the letter "A".

6. El, la, los and las are very important words. They all mean "the". They are the clues you need to tell you a word's category.

El (masculine category – singular)          El niño, El muchacho
Los (masculine category – plural)          Los niños, Los muchachos
La (feminine category – singular)          La niña, La muchacha
Las (feminine category – plural)          Las niñas, Las muchachas

## A Word about Adjectives

In Spanish, most common, descriptive words or adjectives come after the nouns they describe. Conversationally, this is going to require some practice. While you are learning, don't be too concerned about misplacing an adjective or failing to change its final letter to match the noun's category. These are the kinds of common mistakes that everyone makes— even native speakers.

Where the position of adjectives is concerned, there are some notable exceptions. Numbers and other adjectives which show quantity usually come before the noun they describe. That's the way we do it in English!

Descriptive words match the noun by both category and number.

La casa bonita or las casas bonitas

### Tips & Tidbits

Always remember that learning the word is the most important thing, not which category it is! When you are trying to say something, small words like "el" or "la" only mean the. They don't give any clues to what you are trying to say to the person that you are speaking with. Learning the fine points of grammar can wait until you are a master of survival Spanish. First, concentrate on learning the words you need to know!

**ADJECTIVE Describes a noun**

# Descriptions or Descripciones

Describing things in Spanish can present problems for English speakers. There are three reasons why this gives us trouble. First, there is the location of the adjective. In English, descriptive words go in front of the noun like white cat, for example. In Spanish, the noun is the most important element, so it comes first (*gato blanco*). However, it gets a little more complicated because there are a few adjectives that are placed before the noun- and they are very common: For example: large or *grande* (*grande gato blanco*). Next, since Spanish nouns are divided into masculine and feminine categories, the descriptive word should match it by category and by number (singular or plural). This leads us to challenge number three: changing the spelling of the adjective. You might need to change a final "o" to an "a" to change the category. Here is a list of descriptive words that can be used in almost any profession.

| English | Español | English | Español |
|---------|---------|---------|---------|
| **Alive** | Vivo | **Dead** | Muerto |
| **Good** | Bueno | **Bad** | Malo |
| **Better** | Mejor | **Worse** | Peor |
| **Big** | Grande | **Small** | Pequeño |
| **Clean** | Limpio | **Dirty** | Sucio |
| **Hot** | Caliente | **Cold** | Frío |
| **Sane** | Cuerdo | **Crazy** | Loco |
| **Safe** | Seguro | **Dangerous** | Peligroso |
| **Easy** | Fácil | **Difficult** | Difícil |
| **Full** | Lleno | **Empty** | Vacío |
| **Fast** | Rápido | **Slow** | Lento |
| **Hard** | Duro | **Soft** | Blando |
| **New** | Nuevo | **Old** | Viejo |
| **Rich** | Rico | **Poor** | Pobre |
| **Pretty** | Bonito | **Ugly** | Feo |
| **Quiet** | Tranquilo | **Restless** | Inquieto |
| **Tall** | Alto | **Short** | Bajo |
| **Well** | Bien | **Sick** | Enfermo |
| **Strong** | Fuerte | **Weak** | Débil |

# The Essentials of Spanish Verbs

There are basically three types of regular verbs in Spanish. The last two letters on the end of the verb determines how it is to be treated.

Listed below are the three most common types of regular verb endings.

- ✓ AR - Hablar – to speak
- ✓ ER - Comprender – to understand
- ✓ IR - Vivir – to live

In Survival Spanish, we are going to focus on talking about ourselves and talking to another person. That's the most common type of "one on one" communication.

When you want to say I speak, I understand, or I live, change the last two letters of the verb to an "O".

- ✓ Hablo
- ✓ Comprendo
- ✓ Vivo

When asking a question, such as do you speak, do you understand, or do you live, change the ending to an "A" or an "E". The change in letter indicates that you are speaking to someone else.

- ✓ Habla
- ✓ Comprende
- ✓ Vive

To make a sentence negative, simply put "no" in front of the verb.

- ✓ No hablo
- ✓ No comprendo
- ✓ No vivo

**VERB** Shows action or state of being

# ¡Acción!

There are so many English friendly acción words in the Spanish "AR" verb family. Many of them bear a strong resemblance to English verbs- and most of them share a simple, regular nature. They are a very important asset in on-the-job communication. We picked a few of our favorites to get you started. Look closely at the list on page 28. On it, you will recognize many comforting similarities between our languages that are practical too! Changing one letter will really expand your conversational skills.

In on-the-job conversations, people tend to use "I" and "you" to start many sentences. Of all the pronouns, these two are the most powerful and will work the hardest for you. So, that's where we'll start.

Here's an important difference between our languages. In English, the use of pronouns is essential because most of our verbs end the same way. For example, with I speak and you speak; speak remains the same. Our pronouns make all the difference. This isn't true in Spanish. Spanish-speaking people are listening for the letter on the end of the verb. That's what indicates who or what is being talked about. In most cases, you might not hear a pronoun. That's another reason that Spanish might sound a little fast to you: A whole series of words that are important in English are routinely eliminated in Spanish!

Try this: Treat the verbs in the "AR" family as you would "to speak" or "hablar." End the verb with an "o" when you're talking about yourself; "hablo" or "I speak". Change the verb ending from an "o" to an "a" for "habla" or "you speak." Use this form when you're talking to someone else.

| English | Español | Guide |
|---------|---------|-------|
| I need | Necesito | nay-say-**SEE**-toe |
| You need | Necesita | nay-say-**SEE**-ta |

\*\*Note: To make a sentence negative, say no in front of the verb. No necesito. No necesita.

# The Sweet 16 Verbs

| English | Español | Guide |
|---|---|---|
| 1. To need | Necesitar | nay-say-see-**TAR** |
| 2. To use | Usar | oo-**SAR** |
| 3. To prepare | Preparar | pray-pa-**RAR** |
| 4. To clean | Limpiar | limp-e-**ARE** |
| 5. To work | Trabajar | tra-baa-**HAR** |
| 6. To apply | Aplicar | ah-plea-**CAR** |
| 7. To call | Llamar | ya-**MAR** |
| 8. To look for | Buscar | boos-**CAR** |
| 9. To inspect | Inspeccionar | een-speck-see-on-**NAR** |
| 10. To ask | Preguntar | prey-goon-**TAR** |
| 11. To carry | Llevar | yea-**VAR** |
| 12. To repair | Reparar | ray-pa-**RAR** |
| 13. To show | Mostrar | mos-**TRAR** |
| 14. To empty | Vaciar | va-see-**ARE** |
| 15. To pay | Pagar | pa-**GAR** |
| 16. To return | Regresar | ray-grey-**SAR** |

**The "Sweet 16 Verbs" were suggested by participants in SpeakEasy Spanish programs.

Which verbs in the Sweet 16 do you use most often? List your top six:

1. _____

2. _____

3. _____

4. _____

5. _____

6. _____

*Now take your top six, change the AR ending to an "a" and make a negative sentence by adding no at the beginning. For example: No necesita. I don't need.*

1. _____

2. _____

3. _____

4. _____

5. _____

6. _____

*Which verbs would you like to see on the list? Write them below:*

1. _____

2. _____

3. _____

4. _____

5. _____

6. _____

## Tips & Tidbits

On your journey to Spanish proficiency, make prioritizing your vocabulary your ***número uno prioridad***! Go through the "sweet 16" verb list in the table above with different colors of markers. Highlight your "A" list in your favorite color. Look at the vocabulary that remains. Go through it again with a different color- one you don't like so much, and make it your "B" list. Don't begin on your "B" list until you are comfortable with your first choices.

## Para Practicar

*Use verbs from the Sweet 16 to say the following:*

1. Use _____

2. Don't use _____

3. Prepare _____

4. I need *(Remember: Pronouns are often eliminated in Spanish)*

   _____

5. Ask _____

6. To carry_____

7. I'm looking for_____

8. You observe _____

9. I pay _____

10. Call _____

¡Necesito una breaka!

30

# The Big Five – The Most Importante Irregulares

Now that you have had the opportunity to learn about the tremendous number of verbs that follow regular patterns in Spanish, it's time to take a look at others that don't follow the rules. They are unpredictable, but they are very important. In fact, they reflect some of man's oldest concepts. That's why they tend to be irregular. These words were in use long before language rules and patterns were set. So, here they are: to be (2), to have, to make, and to go. Because they don't follow the rules, you will need to memorize them, but that should be easy because you will use and hear them often.

In Spanish there are two verbs that mean **"to be"**. In English, that's I am, you are, he is, etc. The Spanish version is **ser** and **estar**. **Ser** is used to express permanent things like your nationality or profession. **Estar** is used when talking about location or conditions that change like a person's health.

## Ser

| | |
|---|---|
| Yo **soy** | Nosotros **somos** |
| Tú **eres** | |
| Él **es** | Ellos **son** |
| Ella **es** | Ellas **son** |
| Usted **es** | Ustedes **son** |

## Estar

| | |
|---|---|
| Yo **estoy** | Nosotros **estamos** |
| Tú **estás** | |
| Él **está** | Ellos **están** |
| Ella **está** | Ellas **están** |
| Usted **está** | Ustedes **están** |

The verb **"to have"** in Spanish is **muy importante**. In English we say that we are hot, cold, hungry, thirsty, right, wrong or sleepy, but in Spanish those are conditions that you have. Some of those expressions mean something totally different than you expected if you get the verbs confused, so be careful!

## Tener

| | |
|---|---|
| Yo **tengo** | Nosotros **tenemos** |
| Tú **tienes** | |
| Él **tiene** | Ellos **tienen** |
| Ella **tiene** | Ellas **tienen** |
| Usted **tiene** | Ustedes **tienen** |

In Spanish the verb that means, *"to do"* also means, *"to make."* It's not unusual for one verb to have multiple meanings. There are many expressions that require the use of this verb, but you will use it most when you talk about the weather. That's a safe subject and one that everyone, the world over, discusses! **¿Qué tiempo hace?** What's the weather? **Hace frío.** (It's cold.) **Hace sol.** (It's sunny). **Hace calor.** (It's hot) **Hace viento** (It's windy.). Here's two exceptions: **Está lloviendo.** (It's raining.) and **Está nevando.** (It's snowing.)

## Hacer

| | |
|---|---|
| Yo **hago** | Nosotros **hacemos** |
| Tú **haces** | |
| Él **hace** | Ellos **hacen** |
| Ella **hace** | Ellas **hacen** |
| Usted **hace** | Ustedes **hacen**. |

The last of the big five is perhaps the easiest to use. It's the verb that means, *"to go"*. In Spanish, that's **ir**. It's pronounced like the English word ear. Both in English and in Spanish, we use parts of it to make the future tense, in other words, to talk about things that we are going to do. Look at the parts of ir. Then look back at the parts of the verb ser. Do you notice any similarities?

## Ir

| | |
|---|---|
| Yo **voy** | Nosotros **vamos** |
| Tú **vas** | |
| Él **va** | Ellos **van** |
| Ella **va** | Ellas **van** |
| Usted **va** | Ustedes **van** |

When you want to say something that you are going to do, start with I'm going or voy. Next, insert the word "a" and the basic verb that states what it is that you're going to do. Try it! It's easy. Here are some examples.

| | |
|---|---|
| Voy a visitar a mi familia. | I am going to visit my family. |
| Voy a organizar los trabajadores. | I am going to organize the workers. |
| Mario va a comprar las plantas. | Mario is going to buy the plants. |

**The whole concept of irregular verbs is can be quite daunting. Don't let it defeat you! We have many verbs like this in English. In fact, every language has them. The only way to master them is to practice by using them. Make them your own! Try writing different parts of a verb on your desk calendar. That way, it will be there in front of you every time you look down. When you see it, say it to yourself. Then, you'll have it conquered in no time.

## Para Practicar

*Using what you've learned in the preceding chapters, write these phrases in español.*

1. I am going to work. _____

2. I am going to finish. _____

3. Where is Ramón? _____

4. Where is Carlos? _____

5. I am Tim. _____

6. He is Alan. _____

7. She is Amy. _____

8. I have five sisters. _____

9. He has three brothers. _____

10. Juan has four children. _____

*To check your answers, look for the answer key at the back of the book.*

# Los Números How Much - ¿Cuánto?

| Number | Español | Pronunciation Guide |
|---|---|---|
| 0 | Cero | **SAY**-row |
| 1 | Uno | **OO**-no |
| 2 | Dos | dose |
| 3 | *Tres* | trays |
| 4 | Cuatro | coo-**AH**-trow |
| 5 | Cinco | **SINK**-oh |
| 6 | Seis | **SAY**-ees |
| 7 | Siete | see-**A**-tay |
| 8 | Ocho | **OH**-cho |
| 9 | Nueve | new-**A**-Vay |
| 10 | Diez | dee-**ACE** |
| 11 | Once | **ON**-say |
| 12 | Doce | **DOSE**-a |
| 13 | Trece | **TRAY**-say |
| 14 | Catorce | ca-**TOR**-say |
| 15 | Quince | **KEEN**-say |
| 16 | Diez y seis | dee-**ACE**-e-**SAY**-ees |
| 17 | Diez y siete | dee-**ACE**-e-see-**ATE**-tay |
| 18 | Diez y ocho | dee-**ACE**-e-**OH**-cho |
| 19 | Diez y nueve | dee-**ACE**-e-new-**A**-vay |
| 20 | Veinte | **VAIN**-tay |
| 21 | Veinte y uno | **VAIN**-tay -e-**OO**-no |
| 22 | Veinte y dos | **VAIN**-tay -e- dose |
| 23 | Veinte y tres | **VAIN**-tay -e- trays |
| 24 | Veinte y cuatro | **VAIN**-tay -e- Coo-**AH**-trow |
| 25 | Veinte y cinco | **VAIN**-tay -e- **SINK**-oh |
| 26 | Veinte y seis | **VAIN**-tay -e-**SAY**-ees |
| 27 | Veinte y siete | **VAIN**-tay -e- see-**A**-tay |
| 28 | Veinte y ocho | **VAIN**-tay -e **OH**-cho - |
| 29 | Veinte y nueve | **VAIN**-tay -e- new-**A**-vay |
| 30 | Treinta | **TRAIN**-ta |
| 40 | Cuarenta | kwah-**RAIN**-ta |
| 50 | Cincuenta | seen-**KWAIN**-ta |
| 60 | Sesenta | say-**SAIN**-ta |
| 70 | Setenta | say-**TAIN**-ta |
| 80 | Ochenta | oh-**CHAIN**-ta |
| 90 | Noventa | no-**VAIN**-ta |
| 100 | Cien | see-**IN** |
| 200 | Doscientos | dose-see-**N**-toes |
| 300 | Trescientos | tray-see-**N**-toes |
| 400 | Cuatrocientos | coo-**AH**-troh-see-**N**-toes |
| 500 | Quinientos | keen-e-**N**-toes |
| 600 | Seiscientos | **SAY**-ees-see- **N**-toes |
| 700 | Setecientos | **SAY**-tay-see- **N**-toes |
| 800 | Ochocientos | **OH**-choh- see- **N**-toes |
| 900 | Novecientos | **NO**-Vay-see- **N**-toes |
| 1,000 | Mil | meal |

# The Days of the Week and the Months of the Year
## Los Días de la Semana y los Meses del Año

### Los Días de la Semana

| English | Español | Guide |
|---------|---------|-------|
| Monday | lunes | **LOON**-ace |
| Tuesday | martes | **MAR**-tays |
| Wednesday | miércoles | me-**AIR**-co-lace |
| Thursday | jueves | **WAVE**-ace |
| Friday | viernes | v-**AIR**-nace |
| Saturday | sábado | **SAH**-ba-doe |
| Sunday | domingo | doe-**MING**-go |

*It's important to remember when expressing a date in Spanish give the number of the day first followed by the month. Use this format: El (date) de (month).*

### Los Meses del Año

| English | Español | Guide |
|---------|---------|-------|
| January | enero | n-**NAY**-row |
| February | febrero | fay-**BRAY**-row |
| March | marzo | **MAR**-so |
| April | abril | ah-**BRILL** |
| May | mayo | **MY**-oh |
| June | junio | **WHO**-knee-oh |
| July | julio | **WHO**-lee-oh |
| August | agosto | ah-**GOSE**-toe |
| September | septiembre | sep-t-**EM**-bray |
| October | octubre | oc-**TOO**-bray |
| November | noviembre | no-v-**EM**-bray |
| December | diciembre | dee-see-**EM**-bray |

Your job starts (*day of the week*) el (*number*) de (*month*).
*Su empleo comienza lunes, el 11 de octubre.*

Your appointment is Monday the 5th of May.
*Su cita es lunes el cinco de mayo.*

# Practicing Numbers & Dates

*Practice these important items by using numbers, days of the week, and months of the year:*

✓ Your social security number

✓ Your driver's license number

✓ The numbers in your address

✓ Your zip code

✓ Your phone number

✓ Your birth date

✓ Your children's birth dates

✓ The dates of holidays

✓ License tags of the cars in front of you, when you are stopped in

traffic. Combine the Spanish alphabet with this exercise.

✓ Phone numbers you see on billboards

✓ Numbers found on street signs

✓ Phone numbers when you dial them at work or at home

✓ The appointments on your personal calendar

✓ Your wedding anniversary

✓ The dates of all your Spanish classes or practice sessions

# Los Pies y Las Pulgadas
## Feet and Inches

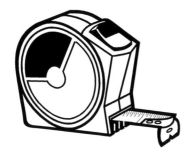

| | |
|---|---|
| Un pie | A foot |
| Una pulgada | An inch |
| Una yarda | A yard |

*A tape measure*
**La cinta métrica or un metro**

*A measurement*
**Una medida**

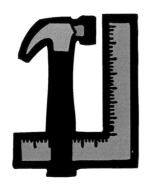

| | |
|---|---|
| 1/16" | Un decimosexto de pulgada |
| 1/8" | Un octavo de pulgada |
| 1/4" | Un cuarto de pulgada |
| 1/2" | Una media de pulgada |
| 3/4 | Tres cuartos de pulgada |

*T-square*
**La escuadra**

*A board 6 feet long and 4 inches wide*
**Una tabla seis pies de larga y cuatro pulgadas de ancha.**

*6 feet long*                                    *4 inches wide*
**Seis pies de larga**                    **cuatro pulgadas de ancha**

| | | | |
|---|---|---|---|
| *Smaller* | **más pequeño** | *Darker* | **más oscuro** |
| *Longer* | **más largo** | *More* | **más** |
| *Shorter* | **más corto** | *Less* | **menos** |
| *Lighter* | **más claro** | | |

# ¿Qué Hora Es?
## What Time Is It?

The concept of time varies from culture to culture.  Many countries put much less emphasis on **always** being on time than Americans do. To Latin Americans p**untualidad** is much more **importante** in the workplace than on social occasions.

*¿Qué hora es?* means **what time is it**?

| | |
|---|---|
| It's one o'clock. | **Es la una.** |
| It's two o'clock. | **Son las dos.** |
| It's 3:30. | **Son las tres y media.** |
| It's 5:45. | **Son las seis menos quince.** |

Use the phrases *de la mañana* to indicate morning and *de la tarde* to indicate afternoon or early evening. Also midnight is *medianoche*.  Noon is *mediodía*.

To find out at what time something takes place ask:    *¿A qué hora…?*

| | |
|---|---|
| **¿A qué hora es la reunión?** | **What time is the meeting?** |
| **¿A qué hora termina?** | **What time do you finish?** |

Spanish speakers sometimes use the 24-hour clock for departures and arrivals of trains and flights, etc.

| | |
|---|---|
| 12.05 | las doce cero cinco |
| 17.52 | las diez y siete cincuenta y dos |
| 23.10 | las veinte y tres diez |
| 07.15 | las siete quince |

## Para Practicar

1. Using the word for meeting, (*la reunion*), say that the meeting takes place on the hour throughout your regular workday. *La reunión es a las ocho.*
2. Tell Sr. Rojas what time your store opens and closes.
3. Using the days of the week and the time to explain a work schedule. Your work schedule is…. *Su horario es…..*

*See answer key*

38

# The Questions Everyone Should Know

| English | Español | Guide |
|---------|---------|-------|
| Who? | ¿Quién? | key-**N** |
| Whose? | ¿De quién? | day key-**N** |
| What? | ¿Qué? | kay |
| Which? | ¿Cuál? | coo-**ALL** |
| When? | ¿Cuándo? | **KWAN**-doe |
| Where? | ¿Dónde? | **DON**-day |
| Why? | ¿Por qué? | pour **KAY** |
| How? | ¿Cómo? | **CO**-mo |
| What's happening? | ¿Qué pasa? | kay **PA**-sa |
| What happened? | ¿Qué pasó? | kay **PA**-so |
| How much? | ¿Cuánto? | **KWAN**-toe |
| How many | ¿Cuántos? | **KWAN**-toes |

When you ask a question in Spanish, it will take on the same form as it does in English. Start with the question word that asks the information you need. Follow the interrogative word with a verb, and give your voice an upward inflection.

In Spanish you can also make a question by ending your sentence with ¿no? Here's an example: Cancún está en México, ¿no? When you end a sentence with "no" like this, it takes on the meaning of "isn't it."

## The Most Common Questions

How are you?  ¿Cómo está?
How much does it cost?  ¿Cuánto cuesta?
Where are you from?  ¿De dónde es?
How old are you?  ¿Cuántos años tiene?

Did you notice the upside down question mark (¿) at the beginning of each question? All questions in Spanish begin with this punctuation mark. All exclamatory phrases like, Hi! Begin with an upside down exclamation point like this: ¡Hola! You can do this on your word processor. Refer to "Typing in Spanish with Microsoft Word" in your table of contents for details.

# Getting the Información
## La entrevista – The Interview

Listed below are the most common questions used during an interview. It's not always necessary to make a complete sentence to have good communication. The information you are asking for is much more important than the phrase "what is your"? As long as you remember to make what you say *sound* like a question by giving your voice an *upward* inflection, people will interpret what you've said *as* a question. Use the form on the following page. Work with a partner to practice giving and receiving information. Make up new answers about yourself for each practice session. You will always be asking the same questions, but the answers you get will always be different!

**What's your. . .**   **¿Cuál es su. . .**
*Coo-ALL ace sue*

| English | Español |
|---|---|
| Full name | Nombre completo |
| First name | Primer nombre |
| Last name | Apellido |
| Paternal surname | Apellido paterno |
| Maternal surname | Apellido materno |
| Address | Dirección |
| Apartment number | Número de apartamento |
| Age | Edad |
| Date of birth | Fecha de nacimiento |
| Nationality | Nacionalidad |
| Place of birth | Lugar de nacimiento |
| Place of employment | Lugar de empleo |
| Occupation | Ocupación |
| Home telephone number | Número de teléfono de su casa |
| Work telephone number | Número de teléfono de su empleo |
| Marital status | Estado civil |
| Driver's license number | Número de licencia |
| Social security number | Número de seguro social |

# Información Básica

Fecha: _____
          Mes      Día      Año

**Sr.**
**Sra.**
**Srta.** _____
     *Primer Nombre    Segundo Nombre    Apellido Paterno    Apellido Materno (Esposo)*

**Dirección:** _____
                              *Calle*

_____
*Ciudad*                    *Estado*              *Zona postal*

**Teléfono: Casa** _____     **Empleo** _____

         **Cel** _____     **Fax** _____

**Correo electrónico** _____

**Número de seguro social:** _____ - _____ - _____

**Número de identificación de contribuyente (TIN):** _____

**Fecha de nacimiento** _____
                         Mes     Día     Año

**Número de la licencia:** _____

**Ocupación:** _____

**Lugar de empleo** _____

**Estado civil:**     Casado (a)
                      Soltero (a)
                      Divorciado (a)
                      Separado (a)
                      Viudo (a)

**Nombre de esposo:** _____
          *Primer Nombre      Segundo Nombre   Apellido Paterno      Apellido Materno*

**Nombre de esposa:** _____
     *Primer Nombre      Segundo Nombre   Apellido Paterno      Apellido Materno/Esposo*

**En caso de emergencia:** _____  **Teléfono:** _____

**Firma:** _____  **Fecha:** _____

41

# The Family – La Familia

Family values are extremely important to Latinos. This is something all of us have in common. Many Latinos have left their families in their native countries to come here for economic reasons. No sacrifice is too great for *la familia*.

Children are considered to be precious gifts. Wives, mothers and grandmothers are greatly respected. Remember that all Hispanics have their mother's surname or *materno apellido*. You are going to hear members of the family from your Hispanic customers. It's something all of us like to talk about!

| English | Español | Guide |
|---|---|---|
| Aunt | Tía | **TEE**-ah |
| Uncle | Tío | **TEE**-oh |
| Brother | Hermano | air-**MAN**-oh |
| Sister | Hermana | air-**MAN**-ah |
| Brother-in-law | Cuñado | coon-**YA**-doe |
| Sister-in-law | Cuñada | coon-**YA**-da |
| Child | Niño, niña | **KNEE**-nyo, **KNEE**-nya |
| Cousin | Primo, prima | **PRE**-mo, **PRE**-ma |
| Daughter | Hija | **E**-ha |
| Son | Hijo | **E**-ho |
| Daughter-in-law | Nuera | new-**AIR**-rah |
| Son-in-law | Yerno | **YEAIR**-no |
| Father | Padre | **PA**-dray |
| Mother | Madre | **MA**-dray |
| Father-in-law | Suegro | soo-**A**-grow |
| Mother-in-law | Suegra | soo-**A**-gra |
| Granddaughter | Nieta | knee-**A**-tah |
| Grandson | Nieto | knee-**A**-toe |
| Grandfather | Abuelo | ah-boo-**A**-low |
| Grandmother | Abuela | ah-boo-**A**-la |
| Husband | Esposo | es-**PO**-so |
| Wife | Esposa | es-**POE**-sa |

## Para Practicar

Using the verb *tener* (to have), tell your practice partner how many relatives you have in your family. Start like this: *Tengo* or I have. Follow that with the number and the member of the family that you are talking about. You will find more about *tener* in the next chapter. Even though it isn't a regular verb, it's very practical. You will use it in many different ways.

## En mi familia.....
*Write the following sentences in Spanish.*

1. I have two sons. _____

2. I have three daughters _____

3. He has four cousins _____

4. My wife has five cousins _____

5. My wife's name is _____

6. I have three uncles _____

7. I have six aunts _____

8. I have no brothers _____

9. I have one (una) sister _____

10. She has no children_____ _____

**\*\*In this exercise use the word "mi" for "my."**

*\*See answer key*

# Employee Benefits & Human Resources
## *Beneficios y Recoursos Humanos*

Go slowly when explaining benefit packages to your Hispanic employees. The whole concept of tax deductions, insurance deductions, and even overtime could be completely new.

| English | Español | Guide |
|---|---|---|
| Benefits | Beneficios | ben-nay-**FEE**-see-ohs |
| Check | Cheque | **CHEC**-kay |
| Disability | Incapacidad | n-ka-pah-see-**DAD** |
| Green card | Tarjeta de residencia | tar-**HEY**-ta day ray-see-**DEN**-cee-a |
| Holidays | Días festivos | **DEE**-ahs fes-**TEE**-vos |
| Insurance | Seguro | say-**GOO**-row |
| License | Licencia | lee-**SEN**-see-ah |
| Medical Insurance | Seguro médico | say-**GOO**-row **MAY**-dee-co |
| Overtime | Sobre tiempo | so-bray-tee-**M**-po |
| Paid vacations | Vacaciones pagadas | va-ca-see-**ON**-ace pah-**GA**-das |
| Paycheck | Paga | **PAH**-ga |
| Retirement | Retiro Jubilación | ray-**TEE**-row who-bee-la-see-**ON** |
| Severance pay | Indemnización por despedida | in-dem-knee-za-see-**ON** pour days-pay-**DEE**-dah |
| Sick leave | Días pagados por enfermedad | **DEE**-ahs pah-**GA**-dos pour in-fer-me-**DAD** |
| Social security | Seguro social | say-**GOO**-row so-see-**AL** |
| Taxes | Impuestos | em-poo-**ACE**-toes |
| Tax deductions | Deducciones de impuestos | day-dook-see-**ON**-aces day em-poo-**ACE**-toes |
| Unemployment Insurance | Seguro de desempleo | say-**GOO**-row day dase-em-**PLAY**-oh |
| Worker's Compensation | Compensación de obrero | com-pen-za-see-**ON** day o-**BRAY**-row |

# Employee Motivation — Motivación de Empleados

All of your employees appreciate your efforts to encourage and motivate them. This is a positive aspect of your position within the company. Doesn't it give you a good feeling to be able to encourage and reward good work with positive comments? Let your Hispanic employees know how much you appreciate their hard work and determination. A big smile and a handshake will go a long way when you use these phrases.

| English | Español | Guide |
|---|---|---|
| It's .....! | ¡Es....! | es |
| Excellent | Excelente | x-see-**LEN**-tay |
| Fantastic | Fantástico | fan-**TAS**-tee-co |
| Good | Bueno | boo-**WAY**-no |
| Extraordinary | Extraordinario | x-tra-or-dee-**NAR**-ree-oh |
| Magnificent | Magnífico | mag-**KNEE**-fee-co |
| What good work! | ¡Qué buen trabajo! | kay boo-**WAYNE** tra-**BAA**-ho |
| Very good! | ¡Muy bien! | mooy b-**N** |
| You're very important! | ¡Usted es muy importante! | oo-**STED** es mooy m-por-**TAN**-tay |
| You're very professional. | ¡Usted es muy profesional! | oo-**STED** es mooy pro-fes-see-on-**NAL** |
| You learn quickly. | Aprende rápido. | ah-**PREN**-day **RAH**-pee-doe |
| I respect you. | Le respeto. | lay race-**PAY**-toe |
| You are very valuable. | ¡Usted es valioso! | oo-**STED** es val-ee-**OH**-so |
| There is… | Hay... | eye |
| Advancement | Ascenso | ahs-**SEN**-so |
| Opportunity | Oportunidad | oh-por-too-knee-**DAD** |
| Great potential | Gran potencial | gran po-ten-see-**AL** |
| Obvious progress | Progreso obvio | pro-**GRES**-oh ob-**VEE**-oh |
| Positive Feedback | Reacción positiva | ray-ax-see-**ON** po-see-**TEE**-va |
| Realistic goals | Metas posibles | **MAY**-tas po-**SEE**-blays |

## Para Practicar

*You are preparing to evaluate one of your best employees. He speaks Spanish along with some English. What phrases will you use to tell him he does good work and you believe he has potential within your organization? You also want to tell him that is very valuable because among other reasons, he learns very quickly. Write the phrases you need in the space provided below.*

1. _____

2. _____

3. _____

4. _____

5. _____

6. _____

7. _____

8. _____

9. _____

10. _____

# Employee Evaluations — Evaluación de Empleados

Helping employees evaluate their job performance helps any business function with better efficiency. Employee performance appraisals occur at regular intervals and are important for both the employee and the employer. The employee should know both strengths and areas that need improvement. After you study this section, review your company's employee evaluation form. Start a form in Spanish to help you prepare for these important conversations.

| English | Español | Guide |
|---|---|---|
| The company needs to evaluate | La compañía necesita evaluar | la com-pa-**KNEE**-ah nay-say-**SEE**-ta a-val-oo-**ARE** |
| Goals | Metas | **MAY**-tas |
| Objectives | Objetivos | ob-hey-**TEE**-vos |
| Strengths | Puntos fuertes | **POON**-toes foo-**AIR**-tays |
| Weaknesses | Debilidades | day-bee-lee-**DAD**-aces |
| Ability | Habilidad | ah-bee-lee-**DAD** |
| Communication | Comunicación | co-moo-knee-ca-se-**ON** |
| Control | Control | con-**TROL** |
| Knowledge | Conocimiento | co-no-see-me-N-toe |
| Language | Lenguaje | len-goo-**AH**-hey |
| Potential | Potencial | po-ten-see-**AL** |
| Talent | Talento | ta-**LEN**-toe |
| The company needs to improve | La compañía necesita mejorar | la com-pa-**KNEE**-ah nay-say-**SEE**-ta may-hor-**RARE** |
| Production | Producción | pro-duke-see-**ON** |
| Quality | Calidad | ca-lee-**DAD** |
| Service | Servicio | ser-**VEE**-see-oh |
| Operation | Operación | oh-pear-rah-see-**ON** |

# Discussing "Problemas"

One of the hardest parts of an employer's job is evaluating employee performance and discussing sensitive subjects. This can be particularly stressful when you are nervous about challenging the language barrier. Before you tackle this situation do some planning first. Think about what you need to say and write a short script in Spanish. Your "cue" cards will help you and give you more confidence. Try not to wait until the last minute to pull this together. The more time that you give yourself to practice, the better your meeting will go. Make sure to save your notes, too. At some point, you may need them again or want to make additions or corrections. Here is a list of words and phrases to get you started.

| English | Español | Guide` |
|---|---|---|
| There is a problem with your | Hay un problema con su… | ay oon pro-**BLA**-ma con sue |
| Absences | Ausencias | ow-**SEN**-see-ahs |
| Using alcohol | Usando el alcohol | oos-**AN**-doe el al-co-**HOL** |
| Attitude | Actitud | ac-tee-**TUDE** |
| Conflict | Conflicto | con-**FLICK**-toe |
| Crime | Crimen | **CREE**-men |
| Drugs | Drogas | **DRO**-gas |
| Harassment | Acosamiento | ah-cos-ah-me-**N**-toe |
| Illness | Enfermedad | n-fair-me-**DAD** |
| Injury | Trauma | tra-**OW**-ma |
| Tardiness | Tardanzas | tar-**DAN**-sas |
| Lack of transportation | Falta de transporte | **FALL**-ta day trans-**POOR**-tay |
| Lack of English proficiency | Falta de competencia en el inglés | **FALL**-ta-day com-pee-**TEN**-see-ah n el eng-**LACE** |
| Personal hygiene | Higiene personal | e-he-**N**-ay pear-so-**NAL** |
| Style of clothing | Estilo de ropa | es-**TEE**-low day **ROW**-pa |

| English | Español | Guide` |
|---|---|---|
| Discrimination | Discriminación | dees-cree-me-na-see-**ON** |
| Insubordination | Insubordinación | n-sue-bore-dee-na-see-**ON** |
| Lack of cooperation | Falta de cooperación | **FALL**-ta day co-oh-pear-rah-see-**ON** |
| Misconduct | Mala conducta | **MA**-la con-**DUKE**-ta |
| Fight | Pelea | pay-**LAY**-ah |

## Tips and Tidbits

Employees with different cultural backgrounds will have different attitudes towards work and employers that will have an impact on your management style. According to Eva S. Kras in her book **Management in Two Cultures** (Intercultural Press, 1995) Latin Americans are less likely to report an on-the-job injury than American employees. In many areas south of the border workers are essentially trained to tell the boss what he **wants** to hear rather than what he **needs** to hear. Many Latin Americans fear that they will be fired if they become injured on the job— or if they are handling a piece of equipment that breaks. Training is the key to managing these issues. Use your Spanish to help you build open relationships that keep lines of communication open. Making sure that you know everyone's name and how to pronounce it correctly is a good start. In Latin America greeting individual employees is very important

## Instructions - Instrucciones

Here are some common instructions for the workplace. Remember to always use the word **instructions** rather than **directions**. This could be confusing to some Latinos because the word *dirección* in Español can mean *address*! It's a good idea to ask this simple question: *¿Comprende mis instrucciones?* Also, don't forget to add *por favor* or please to your *instrucciones*!

| English | Español | Guide |
|---|---|---|
| Come here. | Venga aquí. | **VEN**-ga ah-**KEY**. |
| Let's go. | Vámonos. | **VA**-mo-nos |
| Go with him. | Vaya con él. | **VA**-ya con **L** |
| Wait | Espere. | ace-**PEAR**-ray |
| Stop. | Pare. | **PAR**-ray |
| Help me. | Ayúdeme. | ay-**U**-day-may |
| Help him. | Ayúdelo. | ay-**U**-day-low |
| Like this. | Así. | ah-**SEE** |
| Not like this. | Así no. | ah-**SEE** no |
| Show me. | Muéstreme. | moo-**ACE**-tray-may |
| Good. | Bien. | b**N** |
| Point to it. | Indíquelo. | n-**DEE**-kay-low |
| Move that here. | Mueve eso aquí. | moo-wavy **ACE**-so ah-**KEY** |
| Bring me that. | Tráigame eso. | try-**GA**-may **ACE**-toe |
| Give it to me. | Démelo. | **DAY**-may-low |
| To the right | A la derecha. | a la day-**RAY**-cha |
| To the left. | A la izquierda. | a la ees-kay-**AIR**-da |
| Remove these. | Quite estos. | **KEY**-tay **ACE**-toes |
| Pick up all these. | Recoja todo estos. | ray-**CO**-ha **TOE**-dos **ES**-toes |
| Put it there. | Póngalo allí. | **PON**-ga-low ah-**YE** |
| Around | Alrededor | al-ray-day-**DOOR** |
| Inside | Dentro | **DEN**-tro |
| Under | Debajo | day-**BA**-ho |
| Carry this. | Lleve esto. | **YEA**-vay **ACE**-toe |
| Open/close | Abra, cierre | **AH**-bra. C-**EH**-ray |
| Do it now. | Hágalo ahora. | **AH**-ga-low ah-**ORA** |
| Do it later. | Hágalo más tarde. | **AH**-ga-low mas **TAR**-day |
| Here, there | Aquí, allí | ah-**KEY**, ah-**YE** |
| A little, a lot | Un poco, mucho | un **PO**-ko, **MOO**-cho |

## Para Practicar

*Use the phrases above in combination with the appliances and rooms of the house to say the following:*

1. Go with Pablo and help him. _____

2. I need the refrigerator on the right. _____

3. Move the microwave there. _____

4. Please, do it now. _____

5. Remove the bathroom sink. _____

6. Turn off the electricity. _____

7. Turn off the water. _____

8. Go to the living room. _____

9. Work with Esteban. _____

10. Repair the burner please. _____

*See answer key*

# The House - La Casa

Working with Hispanic employees and sub-contractors is going to give you many opportunities to practice your new Spanish skills. In many southeastern states Hispanic labor makes up between 50% and 75% of the construction labor force. As a builder, knowing the parts of the *casa* will be *muy importante*. To learn this important vocabulary, take adhesive note pads and label the parts of your own home or apartment.

| English | Español | Guide |
|---|---|---|
| Attic | Ático | **AH**-tee-co |
| Basement | Sótano | **SO**-tan-oh |
| Bathroom | Baño | **BAN**-yo |
| | Cuarto de | coo-**ARE**-toe day |
| | baño | **BAN**-yo |
| Bath tub | Bañera | ban-**YAIR**-ah |
| | Tina | **T**-nah |
| Bedroom | Dormitorio | dor-me-**TOR**-e-oh |
| | Recámara | ray-**CA**-ma-rah |
| Master bedroom | Dormitorio principal | dor-me-**TOR**-e-oh |
| | | preen-see-**PAL** |
| Cabinet | Gabinete | ga-b-**NET**-tay |
| Carpet | Alfombra | al-**FOAM**-bra |
| Ceiling | Techo | **TAY**-cho |
| Closet | Armario | are-**MAR**-e-oh |
| Den | Estudio | es-**STEW**-dee-oh |
| Dining room | Comedor | come-a-**DOOR** |
| Door | Puerta | pool-**AIR**-ta |
| Driveway | Camino | ca-**ME**-no |
| | de entrada | day n-**TRA**-da |
| Fireplace | Chimenea | che-me-**NAY**-ah |
| Floor | Piso | **PEE**-so |
| Garage | Garaje | gah-**RAH**-hey |
| Hall | Corredor | core-ray-**DOOR** |
| Kitchen | Cocina | co-**SEE**-nah |
| Laundry room | Lavandería | la-vahn-day-**REE**-ah |
| Living room | Salón | sal-**ON** |
| Pantry | Dispensa | d-**SPEN**-sa |
| Pool | Piscina | p-**SEEN**-na |
| | Alberca | al-**BEAR**-ka |
| Shower | Ducha | **DO**-cha |
| Shutter | Contraventana | contra-ven-**TAN**-nah |
| Stairs | Escaleras | es-ka-**LAIR**-rahs |
| Wall | Pared | par-**RED** |
| Window | Ventana | ven-**TAN**-nah |
| Yard | Patio | **PA**-tee-oh |
| | Yarda | yarda, |
| | Césped | **CES**-ped |

# Appliances and Household Items
## ¡Mi casa es su casa!

| English | Español | Guide |
|---|---|---|
| Appliance | Aparato | ah-pa-**RA**-toe |
| Doesn't work | No funciona | no-funk-see-**ON** ah |
| Stove | Estufa | es-**STEW**-fah |
| Burner | Quemador | k-ma-**DOOR** |
| Oven | Horno | **OR**-no |
| Dryer | Secadora | sec-ah-**DOOR**-rah |
| Washer | Lavadora | la-vah-**DOOR**-rah |
| Dishwasher | Lavaplatos | la-va-**PLA**-toes |
| Garbage disposal | Triturador de basura | tree-too-rah-**DOOR** day ba-**SUE**-rah |
| Refrigerator | Refrigerador | ray-free-hair-ah-**DOOR** |
| Freezer | Congelador | con-hel-ah-**DOOR** |
| Ice maker | Fabricador de hielo | fah-bric-**CANT**-ay day ee-**AY**-lo |
| Microwave oven | Microondas | mee-crow-**ON**-das |

## ¿Cuándo? - When

**I am going to fix it**        Voy a repararlo
**Today**        Hoy
**Tomorrow**        Mañana
**Next week**        En la proxima semana
**In the morning**        En la mañana
**In the afternoon**        En la tarde

# Other Household Items

| English | Español | Guide |
|---|---|---|
| Air conditioning | Aire acondicionado | ire-**RAY** ah-con-d-see-own-**AH**-do |
| Cable TV | Televisión por cable | tay-lay-v-see-**ON** por **KA**-blay |
| Carpet | Alfombra Carpeta (*Spanglish*) | al-**FOM**-bra car-**PET**-ah |
| Ceiling fan | Ventilador de techo | ven-t-la-**DOOR** day **TAY**-cho |
| Computer | Computadora | Com-poo-ta-**DOOR**-rah |
| Drain - sewer | Alcantarilla | al-can-tah-**REE**-yuh |
| Drain - water | Desagüe | daze-**AH**-guay |
| Dumpster | Basurero | ba-soo-**RARE**-o |
| Electricity | Electricidad | elect-**TREE**-see-dad |
| Garbage | Basura | bah-**SOO**-rah |
| Garbage can | Cubo de basura | **KOO**-bo day bah-**SOO**-rah |
| Gas | Gas | gahs |
| Grease | Grasa | **GRA**-sa |
| Grill | Parrilla | pah-**REE**-ya |
| Heater | Calentador | ka-**LEN**-ta-**DOOR** |
| Heating | Calefacción | ka-lay-fac-see-ON |
| Heat pump | Bomba de calor | **BOMB**-ba day **KA**-lore |
| Radiator | Radiador | rah-d-ah-**DOOR** |
| Sink - bathroom | Lavabo | **LA**-va-bo |
| Sink - kitchen | Fregadero | fray-ga-**DAY**-row |
| Telephone | Teléfono | tel-**LAY**-fono |
| Thermostat | Termostato | ter-mo-**STAH**-toe |
| Toilet | Váter Inodoro | **VA**-ter en-**OH**-doe-row |
| Toilet bowl | Taza del váter Retrete | **TA**-sa del **VA**-ter ray-**TRAY**-tay |

**Upstairs**          **el piso de arriba**
**Downstairs**          **el piso de abajo**

# The Tools of the Trade

When you attempt to learn a long list of vocabulary, it's easy to get overwhelmed in the process. I always tell my *amigos* that learning a long list of new words is just like learning to eat a steak. That's right! It's hard to eat the whole thing at once, so we cut it into bite-sized pieces. Spanish is learned much the same way. You have to organize the material and prioritize it. Chew on it a little at a time; then move on to the next bite when you are ready. Go at your own pace, and try not to rush the learning process.

To start the process, go over this material using three colors of highlighter. Choose 10 words and highlight them. Make this your "A" list. Take the next color and highlight 10 more words. This is your "B" list. Don't move to your "B" list until you are comfortable with your first set of vocabulary. Learn the vocabulary that is most important to you first, and work your way down the list until you have mastered them all.

When I have a huge list of new words to learn, I write the first 10 on a "sticky" note and put it on the center of my steering wheel. This way, I can review it whenever I'm stopped in traffic. A simple technique like will let you maximize your time and work on your Spanish when you have a spare moment to chew on it just a little more!

| English | Español | Guide |
|---|---|---|
| Ax | Hacha | **AH**-cha |
| Barrel | Barril | bar-**REEL** |
| Blinds | Persianas | pear-see-**ANN**-ahs |
| Blower | Soplador | soap-lad-**DOOR** |
| Board | Tabla de Madera | ta-**BLA** day ma-**DARE**-ah |
| Bolts | Pernos | **PEAR**-nose |
| Box | Caja | **KA**-ha |
| Broom | Escoba | es-**CO**-bah |
| Breathing mask | Mascarilla | mas-ca-**REE**-ya |
| Paint brush | Brocha | **BRO**-cha |

| English | Español | Guide |
|---|---|---|
| Bucket | Cubo | **COO**-bow |
| Cable | Cable | **CA**-blay |
| Can | Lata | **LA**-ta |
| Canvas or tarp | Lona | **LOW**-na |
| Caulk | Sellador | say-**YA**-door |
| Cement block | Bloque de cemento<br><br>Hormigón | **BLOW**-kay day<br>say-**MEN**-toe<br>or-me-**GONE** |
| Chicken wire | Alambrada | ah-lam-**BRA**-da |
| Chisel | Cincel | seen-**CELL** |
| Clamp | Pinza | **PEEN**-sa |
| Compressor | Compresor | com-pres-**OR** |
| Concrete | Concreto | con-**CRAY**-toe |
| Crane | Grúa | **GREW**-ah |
| Crowbar | Barra | **BAR**-ah |
| Cutter | Cortador | core-ta-**DOOR** |
| Clippers | Trasquiladores | tras-key-la-**DOOR**-ace |
| Drill | Barrena, taladro | bar-**A**-na<br>ta-**LA**-drow |
| Drill bit | Broca | **BRO**-ka |
| Edger | Caladora | cal-ah-**DOOR**-ah |
| File | Lima | **LEE**-ma |
| Framing square | Escuadra | es-coo-**RA**-dra |
| Extension cord | Cable de extensión | **CA**-bley day<br>x-ten-see-**ON** |
| Glue | Goma | **GO**-ma |
| Gravel | Grava | **GRA**-ba |
| Hammer | Martillo | mar-**T**-yo |
| Hack saw | Sierra para cortar<br>metal | see-**AIR**-ah **PA**-ra<br>cor-**TAR** may-**TAL** |
| Hoe | Azadón | ah-sa-**DON** |
| Hose | Manguera | man-**GAY**-rah |
| Knife | Navaja | na-**VA**-ha |
| Jack hammer | Perforadora | pear-for-ah-**DOOR**-ah |
| Ladder | Escalera<br>de mano | es-ka-**LAY**-rah<br>day **MAN**-oh |
| Level | Nivel | **KNEE**-vell |
| Light | Luz | loose |

| English | Español | Guide |
|---|---|---|
| Machine | Máquina | **MA**-key-nah |
| Mattock | Talacha | ta-**LA**-cha |
| Miter box | Caja de mitra | **KA**-ha day **ME**-tra |
| Mop | Trapeador | tra-pay-ah-**DOOR** |
| Nails | Clavos | **CLAH**-vos |
| Nuts | Tuercas | too-**AIR**-kas |
| Paint | Pintura | peen-**TOO**-rah |
| Pan | Cacerola | ca-say-**ROW**-la |
| Pencil | Lápiz | **LAH**-pees |
| Pipe | Tubo | **TOO**-bow |
| Plane | Plano | **PLA**-no |
| Plaster | Yeso | **YEA**-so |
| Plasterboard | Tabla de yeso, El drywall, El sheetrock | **TA**-bla day **YEA**-so |
| Pick | Pico | **P**-co |
| Pliers | Alicates | al-lee-**KA**-tays |
| Plywood | Triply *(Spanglish)* Madera laminada | **TREE**-ply ma-**DEAR**-ah la-me-**NA**-da |
| Power saw | Serrucho eléctrico | say-**ROO**-cho ay-**LEC**-tree-co |
| Putty | Masilla | ma-**SEE**-ya |
| Rags | Trapos | **TRA**-pos |
| Rope | Cuerda | coo-**AIR**-da |
| Shovel | Pala | **PA**-la |
| Rock | Piedra | p-**A**-dra |
| Rebar | Varilla | bar-**REE**-ya |
| Ruler | Regla | **RAY**-gla |
| Rake | Rastrillo | ras-**TREE**-yo |
| Sand | Arena | ah-**RAY**-na |
| Sand paper | Papel de lija | pa-**PEL** day **LEE**-ha |
| Saw | Serrucho Sierra | say-**ROO**-cho see-**AIR**-rah |
| Scaffold | Andamio | an-da-**ME**-oh |
| Screwdriver | Destornillador | days-tor-knee-ya-**DOOR** |
| Screws | Tornillos | tore-**KNEE**-yos |
| Solder | Soldadura | sol-da-**DO**-rah |

| English | Español | Guide |
|---|---|---|
| Soldering iron | Plancha de soldar | **PLAN**-cha day sol-**DAR** |
| Staples | Grapas | **GRA**-pas |
| Staple | Engrapadora | en-gra-pa-**DOOR**-ah |
| Scissors | Tijeras | t-**HAIR**-ahs |
| Scraper | Raspador | ras-pa-**DOOR** |
| Shingle | Ripia | **REE**-p-ah |
| Sprinkler | Aspersor | ahs-pear-**SOAR** |
| Steel | Acero | ah-**SAY**-row |
| Steel wool | Lana de acero | **LA**-na day ah-**SAY**-row |
| Stucco | Estuco | es-**STEW**-co |
| Stud | Tachón | ta-**CHON** |
| Tape | Cinta | **SEEN**-ta |
| Adhesive tape | Cinta adhesiva | **SEEN**-ta add-hay-**SEE**-va |
| Tape measure | Cinta para medir | **SEEN**-ta para may-**DEAR** |
| Tar | Brea | **BRAY**-ah |
| Tarpaper | Papel de brea | pa-**PEL** day **BRAY**-ah |
| Telephone | Teléfono | tay-**LAY**-foe-no |
| Thinner | Diluyente | dee-loo-**YEN**-tay |
| Roofing or outdoor tile | Teja | **TAY**-ha |
| Decorative ceramic tile | Cerámica | say-**RAM**-e-ka |
| Tool | Herramienta | air-rah-me-**N**-ta |
| Tool belt | Cinturón de herramienta | seen-to-**RON** day air-rah-me-**N**-ta |
| Tool box | Caja de herramienta | **KA**-ha day air-rah-me-**N**-ta |
| Trowel | Llana | **YA**-na |
| Trash can | Basurero | bah-sue-**RARE**-oh |
| Vacuum cleaner | Aspiradora | ass-pee-rah-**DOOR**-ah |
| Wall paper | Papel tapiz | pa-**PEL TA**-peas |
| Water | Agua | **AH**-goo-ah |
| Wedge | Cuña | **COON**-ya |
| Wheelbarrow | Caretilla | ca-ray-**TEE**-ya |
| Whistle | Pito | **PEE**-toe |
| Wood | Madera | ma-**DAY**-rah |
| Wire | Alambre | al-**AHM**-bray |

| English | Español | Guide |
|---------|---------|-------|
| Wire brush | Cepillo de alambre | say-**P**-yo day al-**AHM**-bray |
| Wrench | Llave de tuercas | **YA**-vay day too-**AIR**-cas |
| Vise | Tornillo de banco | torn-**KNEE**-yo day **BAN**-co |

1. Learn words you use the most first.
2. Focus on 3 words each week.
3. Practice 10 minutes every day.
4. Label items with post-it notes.
5. Practice at work.

# Framing – La Estructura

Construction terms often vary from country to country. Slang terms are as widely used in Latin America as they are in the United States. To help you work with a broad cross-section of Latinos, we have selected terms that are more generic in Spanish. If there is a problem with vocabulary, ask this important question: *¿Cómo se dice en español?*

| English | Español | Guide |
|---|---|---|
| Beam | Viga | **V**-ga |
| Bearing wall | Pared de carga | pa-**RED** day **CAR**-ga |
| Ceiling joist | Viga de techo | **V**-ga day **TAY**-cho |
| Collar tie | Vigueta de amarre | v-**GAY**-ta day ah-**MAR**-ray |
| Cross bridging | Amarre | ah-**MAR**-ray |
| Floor joist | Viga de entre piso | **V**-ga day **N**-tray **P**-so |
| Girder | Viga principal | **V**-ga preen-see-**PAL** |
| Headset | Viga de cabecera | **V**-ga day ca-bay-**SAY**-rah |
| Insulation | Aislamiento | ay-ee-sla-me-**N**-toe |
| Plate | Viga horizontal | **V**-ga or-ee-son-**TAL** |
| Rafter | Viga | **V**-ga |
| Ridge board | Cumbrera | coom-**BRAY**-ra |
| Roof sheathing | Entablando de techo | n-ta-**BLAN**-doe day **TAY**-cho |
| Sill | Soporte | so-**POR**-tay |
| Steel studs | Montantes de acero | mon-**TAN**-tays day ah-**SAY**-row |
| Stud (wooden) | Montantes de madera | mon-**TAN**-tays day ma-**DARE**-rah |
| Sub floor | Subsuelo | soob-**SWAY**-low |
| Truss | Armadura de cubierto | arm-ma-**DOO**-rah day coo-bee-**AIR**-toe |
| Wall | Pared | pa-**RED** |
| Wall sheathing | Entablado de muro | n-ta-**BLAN**-do day **MOO**-row |

# The Roof – El Techo

A roofer or *techador* is a special part of the construction team. The terms below will help you communication with this important team.

| English | Español | Guide |
|---|---|---|
| Chute | Rampa | **RAHM**-pa |
| Cloth | Trapo | **TRAH**-po |
| Counter flashing | Contraplancha de escurrimiento | **CON**-tra-**PLAHN**-cha day es-coo-ree-me-**N**-toe |
| Fabric | Tela | **TAY**-la |
| Felt | Fieltro de techar | fee-**L**-tro |
| Flashing | Plancha de escurrimiento | **PLAHN**-cha day es-coo-ree-me-**N**-toe |
| Gutter | Canalón | ca-na-**LOAN** |
| Insulation | Aislamiento | ice-la-me-**N**-toe |
| Membrane | Membrana | mem-**BRA**-na |
| Metal Flashing | Plancha de escurrimiento metal | **PLAHN**-cha day es-coo-ree-me-**N**-toe may-**TAL** |
| Roof | Techo | **TAY**-cho |
| Roofing cement | Cemento plástico | say-**MEN**-toe **PLAS**-t-co |
| Roofing felt | Tela para aislar el techo | **TAY**-la **PA**-rah ice-**LAR** l **TAY**-cho |
| Roofing nails | Clavos de techo | **CLA**-vos day **TAY**-cho |
| Roofing paper | Papel de asfáltico | **PA**-pel day as-**FAHL**-t-co |
| Sheet Metal | Hojalata | **OH**-ha **LA**-ta |
| Shingles | Ripias | **REE**-p-ahs |
| Slope | Ángulo de inclinación | **AHN**-goo-low day n-clee-na-see-**ON** |
| Wall Flashing | Plancha de escurrimiento para paredes | **PLAHN**-cha day es-coo-ree-me-**N**-toe **PA**-rah pa-**RED**-es |
| Waterproof | Impermeable | m-pear-me-**AH**-blay |

# Dry Wall

Building styles and materials vary from country to country and even across continents. This is largely because of available materials and the cost of materials. Even weather and climate play a role in the selection of materials. Dry wall is rarely used in Central and Latin America. Cinder blocks covered with stucco often form the majority of the structure. Because this material is so rare, you will often hear the Spanglish "el dry wall" used instead of the true Spanish. Have you noticed that sometimes the Spanish word for a particular tool will be several words long? This is because of the specific nature of the Spanish language. Tools are fully described and the name of the tool demonstrates exactly what it does.

| English | Español | Guide |
|---------|---------|-------|
| Drywall | Tabla de piedra<br>Tabla de yeso | **TAH**-bla day p-**AY**-drah<br>**TAH**-bla day **YEA**-so |
| T-square | Escuadra | es-**SQUAD**-rah |
| Nail gun | Pistola | pees-**TOE**-la |
| "Shots" for nail gun | Pólvora | **POL**-vor-ah |
| Utility belt | Tirante | **TEE**-ran-tay |
| Utility knife | Navaja | na-**VA**-ha |
| Mud | Lodo | **LOW**-doe |
| Scaffolding | Andamio | ahn-da-**MEE**-oh |
| C-clamps | Clanes | **KLA**-nase |
| Concrete pin | Clavija de concreto | cla-**V**-ha-day con-**CRAY**-toe |
| Steel pin | Clavija de acero | cla-**V**-ha day ah-**SAY**-row |
| Paste | Cola | **CO**-la |
| A hanger | Colgador | col-gah-**DOOR** |
| A finisher | Finishero | feen-knee-**SHARE**-row |
| Linear feet | Pies lineal | p-**ACE** lean-ay-**AL** |
| To hang | Colgar | col-**GAR** |

## Para Practicar

*Using the work instructions, the numbers and the vocabulary above, practice the following phrases.*

1. You need to hang 5 feet. _____

2. Bring me the paste please. _____

3. Help the painter. _____

4. Where is the T-square? _____

5. I need the nails. _____

6. Bring the nail gun, please. _____

7. Bring two boxes of nails. _____

8. Bring me the extension cord. _____

9. Ten linear feet _____

10. I need 15 concrete pins. _____

*See answer key

*Make your own list of materials here:*

1. _____

2. _____

3. _____

4. _____

5. _____

# Wall Panels – Paneles de Pared

Quality standards must be maintained at the highest level for each wall panel that is manufactured. As you look through the vocabulary list below, choose the vocabulary that makes up the outer most section and learn those first. Then, work your way to the inside. By categorizing the parts and learning a few each week, you can make the job a lot easier.

| English | Español | Guide |
|---------|---------|-------|
| Bottom Cripples | Pies derechos lisiados inferiores | **P**-ays day-**RAY**-chos lee-see-**AH**-does een-fear-ree-**OH**-rays |
| Bottom Plate | Placa inferior | **PLA**-ka een-fear-ree-**OH**-rays |
| Brick Flashing | Tapajuntas para ladrillos | ta-pa-**WHOON**-tas **PA**-ra lad-**REE**-yos |
| Critical Stud | Pie derecho crítico | **PEE**-ay day-**RAY**-cho **CREE**-tee-co |
| Fire Block | Bloqueo contra Incendio | blow-**KAY**-on **CON**-tra een-**SEND**-dee-oh |
| Header | Cabecero | ca-bay-**SAY**-row |
| Inverted Header | Cabecero invertido | ca-bay-**SAY**-row een-ver-**T**-doe |
| Jack | Gato | **GA**-toe |
| Jack Stud | Pie derecho del gato | **PEE**-ay day-**RAY**-cho del **GA**-toe |
| Ladder Tee | T en escalera | tay n es-ka-**LAIR**-ra |
| L Type Corner | Esquina en forma de L | es-**SKI**-na n **FOR**-ma day **L**-ay |
| Rough Opening | Abertura en bruto | ah-bear-**TOO**-ra n **BREW**-toe |
| SBS Corner | Esquina PBP | ace-**SKI**-na pay bay pay |
| Sheathing | Revestimiento | ray-vase-t-me-**N**-toe |

| English | Español | Guide |
|---|---|---|
| Sill | Antepecho de ventana | an-tay-**PAY**-cho day ven-**TAN**-na |
| T-Brace | Contraviento en T | **CON**-tra vee-**N**-toe n tay |
| Top Cripple | Pie derecho lisiado superior | **PEE**-ay day-**RAY**-cho lee-see-**AH**-doe sue-pear-ree-**OR** |
| Top Plate | Placa superior | **PLA**-ka sue-pear-ree-**OR** |
| Trimmer | Placa de ajuste | **PLA**-ka day ah-**WHO**-stay |
| Very Top Plate | Placa de arriba de todo | **PLA**-ka day Ah-**REE**-ba day **TOE**-doe |

## Deck–Terraza

| English | Español | Guide |
|---|---|---|
| Post | Poste | **POE**-stay |
| Decking | Cubierta | coo-bee-**AIR**-ta |
| Concrete post foundation | Poste de hormigón<br><br>Pilote de concreto | **POE**-stay day or-me-**GONE**<br>p-**LOW**-tay day con-**CRAY**-toe |
| Joists | Vigas | **VEE**-gas |
| Stringer | Travesaño | tra-vay-**SAN**-yo |
| Tread | Peldaño | pail-**DAN**-yo |
| Railing | Baranda<br>Barra carril | ba-**RAHN**-da<br>**BAA**-rah ca-**REEL** |

# Stairs–Escaleras

*Using the vocabulary listed below, label the parts of this set of stairs.*

| English | Español | Guide |
|---|---|---|
| Handrail | Pasamano | **PA**-sa-**MA**-no |
| Balusters | Barandilla | baa-ran-**DEE**-ya |
| Skirt Board | Falda | **FAL**-da |
| Return Nosing | Moldure de retorno | mol-**DOO**-ray day ray-**TOR**-no |
| Riser | Contrahuella | **CON**-tra-who-**A**-ya |
| Baseboard | Zócalo | **SO**-ca-low |
| Step | Escalone | ace-ca-**LONE**-ay |
| Nosing | Vuelo | voo-**A**-low |
| Landing | Descanso | des-**CAN**-so |
| Starting Newel | Baranda principal | baa-**RAN**-da preen-see-**PAL** |

# Truss–Armadura

Assembling a truss requires top-notch team work- and specialized skills. Each person in the building crew has different positions and responsibilities. Every part of the process is defined down to the last detail to make efficiency and safety a priority.

Training is also an important part of this manufacturing process. Machinery such as power saws, forklifts, nail guns, and presses may be included in your company's training programs. Your success in this environment will depend on your ability to function as a member of the team. Good communication skills will also make you an even more important member of the team.

| English | Español | Guide |
|---|---|---|
| Bearing | Soporte | so-**POUR**-tay |
| Bottom Chord | Cuerda inferior | coo-**AIR**-da<br>een-fair-ree-**OR** |
| Butt Cut | Corte de tope | **CORE**-tay day<br>**TOE**-pay |
| Camber | Comba | **COMB**-ba |
| Cantilever | Voladizo | vo-la-**DEE**-so |
| Chase | Paso | **PA**-so |
| Fascia Point | Punto de facia | **POON**-toe day<br>**FA**-see-ah |
|  | Punto de frontis | **POON**-toe day<br>**FRON**-tees |
| Girder | Viga maestra | **VEE**-ga ma-**ACE**-tra |
| Heel | Talón | ta-**LAWN** |
| Overhang | Saliente | sa-lee-**N**-tay |
| Panel Length | Largo de panel | **LAR**-go day pan-**L** |
| Panel Point | Punto de panel | **POON**-toe day pan-**L** |
| Peak | Pico | **P**-co |
| Pitch | Pendiente | pen-d-**N**-tay |
| Pitch Break | Interrupción de la pendiente | een-terr-roop-see-**ON**<br>day la<br>pen-d-**N**-tay |

| English | Español | Guide |
|---|---|---|
| Plumb Cut | Corte de plomada | **CORE**-tay day Plo-**MA**-da |
| Scarf Cut | Corte biselado | **CORE**-tay bee-say-**LA**-doe |
| Sea Cut | Corte tipo asiento | **CORE**-tay **TEE**-po ah-see-**N**-toe |
| Stud Spacing | Espacio entre pies derechos | ace-**PA**-see-oh **N**-tray **PEE**-ace day-**RAY**-chos |
| Span | Vuelo | voo-**A**-low |
| Splice | Empalme | m-**PALM**-may |
| Square Cut | Corte de escuadra | **CORE**-tay day es-coo-**AH**-dray |
| Top Chord | Cuerda superior | coo-**AIR**-da soo-pear-ree-**OR** |
| Truss | Armadura | ar-ma-**DOO**-ra |
| Truss Plate | Placa de armadura | **PLA**-ca day ar-ma-**DOO**-ra |
| Web | Red | red |

## Electricity - Electricidad

An electrician or *electricista* has an important and dangerous job. In this specialty good communication is critical. Nothing is more important than making sure each member of the crew is working safely and that parts of the project are up to code.

In this highly technical area, go through the list first and decide which words you will learn first. Always start with the words and phrases that you will use the most.

| English | Español | Guide |
|---|---|---|
| 110 Volts | Voltaje de cien diez | vol-**TA**-hey day<br>see-**N** dee-**ACE** |
| 220 Volts | Voltaje de doscientos veinte | vol-**TA**-hey day<br>dose-see-**N**-toes **VEIN**-tay |
| Air conditioner | Acondicionador | ah-con-dee-see-on-na-**DOOR** |
| Allen Wrench | Llave de tuercas "Allen" | **YA**-vay day two-**AIR**-cas "Allen" |
| Aluminum | Aluminio | al-oo-**ME**-knee-oh |
| Ammeter | Amperímetro | am-pear-**REE**-may-tro |
| Ampere | Amperio | am-**PEAR**-ree-oh |
| Anchors | Áncora | **AHN**-core-rah |
| Breaker Panel | Panel de rompedores | pa-**NAIL** day<br>rom-pay-**DOOR**-aces |
| Brown | Marrón | ma-**RON** |
| Bulb | Bombilla<br>Foco | bomb-**BEE**-ya<br>**FO**-co |
| Cable | Cable | **CA**-blay |
| Ceiling Fan | Ventilador de techo | ven-tee-la-**DOOR**<br>day **TAY**-cho |
| Chandelier | Araña | ah-**RAN**-ya |
| Chime | Campanada | cam-pa-**NA**-da |
| Circuit Breaker | Interruptor automático<br>Cortacircuito | n-ter-roop-**TOR**<br>ow-toe-**MA**-tee-co<br>core-ta-sear-coo-**EE**-toe |
| Code | Código | **CO**-dee-go |
| Concealed | Ocultado | oh-cool-**TA**-doe |
| Conduit Bender | Doblador de cubos | doe-bla-**DOOR**<br>day **COO**-bows |
| Connector | Conector | co-neck-**TOR** |
| Copper | Cobre | **CO**-bray |
| Cutout Box | Caja de cortacircuito fusible | **CA**-ja day<br>core-ta-sear-coo-**EE**-toe<br>foo-**SEE**-blay |
| Cutting Pliers | Alicates de corte<br>Pinzas cortantes | ah-lee-**CA**-tays day **CORE**-tay<br>**PEEN**-sas core-**TAN**-tay |
| Dimmer | Reductor de luz | ray-duke-**TOR** day loose |
| Doorbell | Timbre | **TEAM**-bray |
| Doorbell Button | Botón de timbre | bow-**TON** day **TEAM**-bray |

| English | Español | Guide |
|---|---|---|
| Duct | Conducto porta cables | con-**DUKE**-toe **POR**-ta **CA**-blays |
| Exposed | Exponer | x-pone-**AIR** |
| Fixture | Artefacto | are-tay-**FAC**-toe |
| Flexible Conduit | Tubo-conducto flexible | **TOO**-bow con-**DUKE**-toe flex-**SEE**-blay |
| Fluorescent | Fluorescente | flew-oh-ray-**SEN**-tay |
| Furnace | Horno | **OR**-no |
| Fuse | Fusible | foo-**SEE**-blay |
| Ground | Tierra | tee-**AIR**-rah |
| Ground Clamp | Grampa | **GRAM**-pa |
| Ground Rod | Barra de tierra | **BAR**-rah day tee-**AIR**-rah |
| Hack Saw | Sierra para cortar metales | see-**AIR**-rah **PA**-ra cor-**TAR** may-**TAL**-aces |
| Heater | Calentador | ca-lent-ta-**DOOR** |
| Hole Cutter | Cortador de perforación | cor-ta-**DOOR** day pear-for-rah-see-**ON** |
| Hot | Caliente | ca-lee-**N**-tay |
| Incandescent | Incandescente | n-can-days-**SENT**-tay |
| Insulation | Insolación | n-so-la-see-**ON** |
| Intermediate Conduit | Tubo-conducto intermedio | **TOO**-bow con-**DUKE**-toe n-ter-**MAY**-dee-oh |
| Ivory | Marfil | mar-**FEEL** |
| Ladder | Escalera a mano | ace-ca-**LAIR**-rah ah **MA**-no |
| Level | Nivel | knee-**VEL** |
| Lights | Luz | loose |
| Line | Línea | **LEAN**-nay-ah |
| Live Wire | Alambre vivo | ah-**LAMB**-ray **VEE**-vo |
| Load | Carga | **CAR**-ga |
| Microwave Oven | Microonda | me-crow-**OON**-da |
| Multi meter | Contador múltiple | con-ta-**DOOR** **MOO**-tee-play |
| Neutral | Neutral | nay-oo-**TRAL** |
| Non-Metallic Sheathed Cable | Cable cubierto no metálico | **CA**-blay coo-bee-**AIR**-toe no may-**TAL**-lee-co |
| Off | Apague | ah-**PA**-gay |
| Ohm | Ohmio | **OH**-mee-oh |
| Ohmmeter | Ohmiómetro | oh-mee-**OH**-may-tro |

| English | Español | Guide |
|---|---|---|
| On | Encendido | n-sen-**D**-doe |
| Pipe Threader | Rosca<br>de tubería | **ROWS**-ca<br>day too-bear-**REE**-ah |
| Power | Electricidad | a-leck-tree-see-**DAD** |
| Range (stove) | Estufa | es-**TOO**-fa |
| Receptacle | Receptáculo<br>Caja de contacto | ray-cep-**TA**-coo-low<br>**CA**-ha day con-**TACK**-toe |
| Ridged Conduit | Tubo-conducto sólido | **TOO**-bow con-**DUKE**-toe<br>**SO**-lee-doe |
| Service | Servicio | ser-**VEE**-see-oh |
| Single Phase | Monofásico | mo-no-**FA**-see-co |
| Six Foot Rule | Regla de<br>seis pies | **RAY**-gla day<br>**SAY**-ees **PEE**-ays |
| Skin (Verb) | Despellejar | des-pay-**YEA**-har |
| Smoke Detector | Detector de humo | day-tec-**TOR** day **OO**-mo |
| Splice | Empalmar | em-pahl-**MAR** |
| Staple | Grapa | **GRA**-pa |
| Strip (Verb) | Desaforrar | day-sa-for-**RARE** |
| Switch | Interruptor | en-tay-roop-**TOR** |
| Thermostat | Termostato | tear-moe-**STAT**-o |
| Thin wall<br>Conduit | Tubo-conducto de<br>pared delgado | **TOO**-bow con-**DUKE**-toe day<br>Pa-**RED** del-**GA**-doe |
| Three Phase | Fase de tres | **FA**-see day trays |
| Transformer | Transformador | trans-for-ma-**DOOR** |
| Tube | Tubo | **TOO**-bow |
| Utility Company | Compañía de<br>utilidades | com-pa-**KNEE**-ya day<br>oo-tee-lee-**DAD**-ace |
| Voltmeter | Voltímetro | vol-**TEE**-may-tro |
| Volts | Voltajes | vol-**TA**-heys |
| Washer | Arandela | ah-ran-**DAY**-la |
| Water Heater | Calentador de agua | ca-len-ta-**DOOR** day **AH**-gua |
| Watts | Vatios | **VA**-tee-ohs |
| White | Blanco | **BLAN**-co |
| Wire Nuts | Tuercas<br>de alambre | too-**AIR**-cas<br>day al-**LAMB**-bray |
| Wrench | Llave de tuercas | **YA**-vay day two-**AIR**-cas |

*Brand names are used for items throughout the construction industry. There's no need to translate a brand name like Black & Decker, Caterpillar, John Deere, DeWalt or Irwin.*

# Plumbers–Plomeros

Remember to prioritize your work. Look for the words you use the most and learn them first. Get your Hispanic employees to help you. And, you can help them too by posting five words each week in English and in Spanish in your break room on large poster paper. Everyone can learn together and follow your great example!

| English | Español | Guide |
|---------|---------|-------|
| Auger | Barrena | bar-**RAY**-na |
| Basin | Pila | **PEE**-la |
| Bend | Curva | **COOR**-va |
| Bin | Depósito | day-**POE**-see-toe |
| Broom | Escoba | ace-**CO**-ba |
| Cast iron | Hierro fundido | e-**YAIR**-row foon-**DEE**-doe |
| Clean | Limpia | **LEEM**-pee-ah |
| Cleaner | Limpiador | leem-pee-ah-**DOOR** |
| Crawl space | Espacio debajo de la casa | ace-**SPA**-see-oh day-**BA**-ho day la **CA**-sa |
| Crimper | Plegador de tubos | play-ga-**DOOR** day **TOO**-bows |
| Dishwasher | Máquina lavaplatos | **MA**-key-na lava-**PLA**-toes |
| Disposal | Disposición de las basuras | dees-po-see-see-**ON** day las ba-**SUE**-ras |
| Drain | Desagüe | des-**AH**-gway |
| To drain | desaguar | des-ah-**GUAR** |
| Drainage | Drenaje Desagüe | dran-**NA**-hey; des-**AH**-gway |
| Drain plug | Tapón de evacuación | ta-**PON** day a-va-coo-ah-see-**ON** |

| English | Español | Guide |
|---|---|---|
| Drain area | Área colectora | **AH**-ray-ah co-lec-**TOR**-ah |
| Drain valve | Válvula purgadora de sedimentos | **VAL**-voo-la purr-ga-**DOOR**-ah day say-dee-**MEN**-toes |
| Drain hole | Orficio de purga | or-**FEE**-see-oh day **PURR**-ga |
| Drain pipe | Tubo de desagüe | **TWO**-bow day des-**AH**-gway |
| Drain system | Sistema de drenaje | sis-**TAY**-ma day dray-**NA**-hey |
| Drainage fittings | Accesorios drenables | ah-ces-**ROAR**-ree-ohs dran-**NA**-blays |
| Drill | Taladro | ta-**LA**-drow |
| Drip | Gotero | go-**TAY**-row |
| Drip pan | Recoge gotas | ray-**CO**-hay **GO**-tas |
| Drip ring | Anillo de goteo | ah-**KNEE**-yo day go-**TAY**-oh |
| Drip tight | Prueba de goteo | pru-**A**-ba day go-**TAY**-oh |
| Drop (liquid) | Gota | **GO**-ta |
| Ell | Ele | **AY**-lay |
| Elbow | Codo, Ele | **CO**-doe, ay-lay |
| Escutcheon plate | Escudete de cerradura Escudo | ace-coo-**DAY**-tay day say-ra-**DOO**-ra ace-**COO**-doe |
| Extension cord | Cable de extensión | **CA**-blay day ex-ten-see-**ON** |
| Faucet | Grifo | **GREE**-foe |
| FHA plates | Plato de FHA | **PLA**-toe day **FHA** |
| Fitting | Ajuste | ah-**WHO**-stay |
| Flange | Brida | **BRIE**-da |
| Flow | Flujo | **FLEW**-ho |
| Flux | Fundente | foon-**DEN**-tay |
| Framing | Estructura | es-struck-**TOO**-rah |
| Gauge | Véase | **VAY**-ah-say |
| Glue | Pegamento | Peg-ah-**MEN**-toe |
| Hanging iron | Hierro suspendido | e-**AIR**-row sus-pen-**DEE**-doe |
| Header | Travesaño | tra-vase-**AN**-yo |
| Hole | Perforación | pear-for-rah-see-**ON** |
| Insulation | Aislamiento | ice-la-me-**N**-toe |
| Laundry sink | Pileta de lavar | pee-**LAY**-ta day la-**VAR** |
| Lavatory | Lavabo | **LA**-va-bo |
| Main water | Agua principal | **AH**-gua preen-see-**PAL** |
| Main sewer | Cloaca principal | clo-**AH**-ca preen-see-**PAL** |

| English | Español | Guide |
|---|---|---|
| Mortar | Mortero | more-**TAY**-row |
| Nail guards | Protección de clavos | pro-tec-see-**ON** day **CLA**-vos |
| Nut driver | Entuercadora | n-too-air-ca-**DOOR**-rah |
| Kitchen sink | Fregadero | fray-ga-**DAY**-row |
| Pedestal sink | Lavabo pedestal | la-**VA**-bow ped-day-**STAL** |
| Pipe | Tubo | **TOO**-bow |
| Plug | Tapón | ta-**PON** |
| Plumber | Plomero | plo-**MAY**-row |
| Plumbing | Plomería | plo-may-**REE**-ah |
| Plumbing contractor | Plomero contratista | plo-**MAY**-row con-tra-**TEE**-sta |
| Plumbing fixtures | Artefactos sanitarios | are-tay-**FACT**-toes san-knee-**TAR**-ree-ohs |
| Pressure | Presión | pres-see-**ON** |
| Propane | Propano | pro-**PAN**-oh |
| Pump | Bomba | **BOM**-baa |
| Rack | Casillero | ca-see-**YAIR**-row |
| Ring | Anillo | an-**KNEE**-yo |
| Rough in | Tubería | too-bear-**REE**-ah |
| Safety glasses | Gafas de seguridad | **GA**-fas day say-goo-ree-**DAD** |
| Sewage | Agua negro | **AH**-gooah **NAY**-grow |
| Sewage disposal | Evacuación de las aguas residuales | a-va-coo-ah-see-**ON** day las **AH**-guas res-see-dent-tee-**AL**-ace |
| Sewer | Albañal | al-**BAN**-yall |
| Sewer tap | Boca de admisión | **BO**-ca day add-me-see-**ON** |
| Shower | Baño de ducha | **BAHN**-yo day **DOO**-cha |
| Shower head | Boquilla de ducha | bow-**KEY**-ya day **DOO**-cha |
| Shut off | Válvula de cierre, Válvula de interupción | **VAL**-voo-la day see-**AIR**-ree **VAL**-voo-la day en-tay-rupt-see-**ON** |
| Skill saw | Sierra | see-**AIR**-ah |
| To saw | Serrar | ser-**RAR** |
| Slab | Losa de cimiento | **LOW**-sa day see-**MEE**-en-toe |
| Sleeve | Manguito | man-**GEE**-toe |
| Slope | Inclinación | in-cla-na-see-**ON** |
| Solder | Soldadura | sol-da-**DOO**-rah |
| Steel | Acero | ah-**SAY**-row |

| English | Español | Guide |
|---|---|---|
| Strap | Correa | core-**RAY**-ah |
| Stub out | Desvío muerto | des-**VEE**-oh moo-**AIR**-toe |
| To sweep | Escobar | ace-co-**BAR** |
| Tap | Grifo | **GREE**-foe |
| Tee | Véase T | **VA**-ah-say tay |
| Temperature | Temperatura | tem-pear-ra-**TOO**-rah |
| Toilet bowl | Cisterna | cease-**TER**-na |
| Toilet tank | Tanque de sanitario | **TAN**-kay day san-knee-**TAR**-ree-oh |
| Torch | Soplete de gasolina | so-**PLAY**-tay day gas-oh-**LEAN**-na |
| Trap | Trampa | **TRAM**-pa |
| Trench | Zanja | **SAN**-ha |
| Trim | Contramarcos | con-tra-**MAR**-cos |
| Valve | Válvula | **VAL**-voo-la |
| Vent | Orificio de ventilación | or-ee-**FEE**-see-oh day ven-tee-la-see-**ON** |
| Water heater | Calentador de agua | cal-lent-ta-**DOOR** day **AH**-goo-ah |

## Landscaping & Irrigation

This list contains the most common tools used by landscapers and gardeners. How many of the words listed below do you use every day? As you review the list for the first time, pay close attention to words that are almost the same between English and Spanish. These will be the easiest to learn.

| English | Español | Guide |
|---|---|---|
| Blower | Soplador | so-pla-**DOOR** |
| Chain | Cadena | ca-**DAY**-nah |
| Chain saw | Sierra cadena | see-**AIR**-ah ca-**DAY**-nah |
| Clippers | Cortadora | core-ta-**DOOR**-ah |
| Concrete block | Bloque de cemento | **BLO**-kay day say-**MEN**-toe |
| Containers | Contenedor | con-ten-**A**-door |
| Diesel | Diesel | Same as English |

| English | Español | Guide |
|---|---|---|
| Edger | Caladora | ca-la-**DOOR**-ah |
| Fertilizer | Fertilizante | fur-til-lee-**ZAN**-tay |
| Flowers | Flores | **FLOOR**-rays |
| Gas | Gasolina | gas-so-**LEE**-nah |
| Grease | Grasa | **GRA**-sa |
| Grease Gun | Pistola de grasa | pee-**STOW**-la day **GRA**-sa |
| Hacksaw | Sierra para cortar metal | see-**AIR**-ah **PA**-ra core-**TAR** may-**TAL** |
| Hose | Manguera | man-**GAY**-rah |
| Hose off or water | Regar | **RAY**-gar |
| Irrigation | Irrigación Riego | ear-ree-gah-see-**ON** ree-**A**-go |
| Knife | Navaja | na-**VA**-ha |
| Level | Nivel (tool) | **KNEE**-vel |
| Manure | Abono | ah-**BOW**-no |
| Mattock | Pico | **PEE**-ko |
| Mulch To mulch | Pajote Cubrir con pajote | pah-**HO**-tay Coo-**BREAR** con Pah-**HO**-tay |
| Oil | Aceite | ah-**SAY**-tay |
| Pine needles | Aguja de pino | ah-**GOO**-ha day **PEE**-no |
| Rake | Rastrillo | ras-**TREE**-yo |
| Seed | Semilla | say-**ME**-ya |
| Shovel | Pala | **PAH**-la |
| Sod | Tepe | **TAY**-pay |
| Sod staples | Grapas de tepe | **GRA**-pas day **TAY**-pay |
| Sprayer | Pulverizador | pull-ver-ree-**ZA**-door |
| Spreader | Propagador | pro-pah-**GA**-door |
| Straw | Paja | **PAH**-ha |
| Tamper | Pisón Apisonar | pee-**SON** ah-pee-son-**ARE** |
| Tarp | Lona | **LOW**-na |
| Trailer | Transporte por camión | trans-**POR**-tay pour **KA**-me-**ON** |
| Tree | Árbol | **ARE**-bowl |
| Truck | Camión | **KA**-me-**ON** |

| English | Español | Guide |
|---|---|---|
| Truck bed | Cama de camion | **KA**-ma day **KA**-me-**ON** |
| Truck cab | Interior de camión | n-tear-**REE**-or day ca-me-**ON** |
| Water tank | Tanque de agua | tan-**KAY** de **AH**-goo-ah |
| Weed | Mala hierba | **MA**-la e-**AIR**-bah |
| Weed eater | Escardadora | es-car-dah-**DORA** |
| Weed killer | Herbicida | air-bee-**SEE**-da |
| Wheel | Rueda | roo-**A**-dah |
| Window | Ventana | ven-**TA**-na |
| Wrench | Llave | **YAH**-vay |
| Yard | Césped | **CES**-ped |

## Surveyor's Tools
Las Herramientas de los Topógrafos

| English | Español | Guide |
|---|---|---|
| 100-foot tape | Cinta de cien pies | **SEEN**-ta day see-**N** pee-**ACE** |
| 25-foot tape | Cinta de veinte y cinco pies | **SEEN**-ta day **VAIN**-tay ee **SINK**-oh pee-**ACE** |
| 30-penny nail | Clavo de treinta "pennies" | **CLA**-vow de **TRAIN**-ta Pennies (No kidding!  Nails are measured by "pennies" just like in the US.) |
| 3-pound hammer | Martillo de tres pesos | mar-**TEE**-yo de trays **PAY**-sos |
| Bush ax | Hacha de arbusto | **ACH**-a day are-**BOO**-stow |
| Chain pin | Cadena para medir | ca-**DAY**-na **PA**-ra may-**DEAR** |
| Dock spike | Punta de estaca | **POON**-ta day es-**STACK**-ah |

| English | Español | Guide |
|---|---|---|
| Drafting scale | Escala de esbozo | es-**CA**-la day es-**BOW**-so |
| Equipment cover | Cubierta de equipo | coo-bee-**AIR**-ta day a-**KEY**-poe |
| Flagging | Señalando | sen-yal-**AN**-doe |
| Hub | Cubo | **COO**-bow |
| Instrument | Instrumento | N-strew-**MEN**-toe |
| Irons | Hierros | e-**ARROWS** |
| Level rod | Nivel de barra | knee-**BELL** day **BAR**-rah |
| Level transit | El nivel de tránsito | knee-**BELL** day **TRAN**-sit-toe |
| Magnetic finder | Buscador magnético | boos-ca-**DOOR** mag-**NAY**-tee-co |
| Magnetic nail | Clavo magnético | **CLA**-vow mag-**NAY**-tee-co |
| Marking paint | Pinta de marca | **PEEN**-ta day **MAR**-ca |
| Pin | Clavo grande | **CLA**-vo **GRAN**-day |
| Pin setter | Clavo de marca | **CLA**-vo day **MAR**-ca |
| Plumb bob | Plomo | **PLO**-moe |
| Plumb line | Cuerda de plomada | coo-**AIR**-da day plo-**MA**-da |
| Prism | Prisma | **PREES**-ma |
| Prism pole | Poste de prisma | **POS**-tay day **PREES**-ma |
| Short stakes | Estacas cortas | es-**STACK**-ahs **CORE**-tas |
| Stake bag | Bolsa de estacas | **BOWL**-sa day es-**STACK**-ahs |
| Star drill | Taladro de estrella | ta-**LA**-drow day es-**TRAY**-ya |
| Surveyor | Topógrafo | toe-**POE**-gra-foe |
| Tall stakes | Estacas altas | es-**STACK**-ahs **AL**-tas |
| Tool pouch | Bolsa de herramientas | **BOWL**-sa day hair-rah-me-**N**-tas |
| Tripod | Trípode | **TREE**-po-day |

# Windows and Doors – Ventanas y Puertas

Doors and windows have a variety of small but important parts. To learn this vocabulary, label a door or window in your home. Review the words each evening after work. If you have niños, let them help you make flash cards or practice your vocabulary. Kids make great teachers–especially if they are learning Spanish.

| English | Español | Guide |
|---|---|---|
| **Door** | **Puerta** | **poo-AIR-ta** |
| Bell | Timbre | **TEEM**-bray |
| Bolt | Cerrojo | say-**ROW**-ho |
| Case | Contramarco | **CON**-tra **MAR**-co |
| Check | Cierra puerta | see-**A**-rah poo-**AIR**-ta |
| Frame | Marco de puerta | **MAR**-co day poo-**AIR**-ta |
| Hanger | Suspensor de puerta | sue-spen-**SOAR** day poo-**AIR**-ta |
| Hardware | Herraje de puerta | ay-**RAY**-hey day poo-**AIR**-ta |
| Head | Dintel | deen-**TEL** |
| Holder | Retenedor de puerta | ray-ten-nay-**DOOR** day poo-**AIR**-ta |
| Jamb | Jamba de puerta | **HAHM**-ba day poo-**AIR**-ta |
| Knob | Pomo | **PO**-mo |
| Knocker | Aldaba | ahl-**DA**-ba |
| Leaf | Contrabisagra de puerta | **CON**-tra-bees-**AH**-gra day poo-**AIR**-ta |
| Post | Jamba | **HAHM**-ba |
| Pull | Tirador | t-rah-**DOOR** |
| Step | Escalón de entrada | es-ca-**LOAN** day n-**TRA**-da |
| Sill | Umbral | oom-**BRAL** |
| Stop | Tope | **TOE**-pay |
| Throat | Garganta de puerta | gar-**GAN**-ta day poo-**AIR**-ta |
| Way | Portal | por-**TAL** |

| English Window | Español Ventana | Guide Ven-TA-na |
|---|---|---|
| Bar | Barra de ventana | **BAR**-rah day ven-**TA**-na |
| Blind | Persiana | pear-see-**ANN**-na |
| Fastener | Fiador de ventana | fee-ah-**DOOR** day ven-**TA**-na |
| Frame | Marco de ventana | **MAR**-co day ven-**TA**-na |
| Glass | Vidrio común | **V**-dree-oh co-**MOON** |
| Guard | Salvavidrio | sal-va- **V**-dree-oh |
| Head | Cabezal de ventana | ca-bay-**SAL** day ven-**TA**-na |
| Opening | Vano de ventana | **VA**-no day ven-**TA**-na |
| Pane | Hoja de vidrio Cristal | **OH**-ha day **V**-dree-oh crease-**TAL** |
| Pipe | Tube de descarga | **TOO**-bay day des-**CAR**-ga |
| Sash | Hoja de ventana | **OH**-ha day ven-**TA**-na |
| Screen | Mosquitero | moes-key-**TER**-row |
| Shutter | Contraventana | **CON**-tra-ven-**TA**-na |
| Sill | Umbral de ventana | oom-**BRAL** day ven-**TA**-na |
| Speed | Velocidad del viento | vay-lo-see-**DAD** del v-**N**-toe |
| Stop | Tope de hoja de ventana | **TOE**-pay day **OH**-ha day ven-**TA**-na |
| Trim | Contramarco de ventana | **CON**-tra-**MAR**-co day ven-**TA**-na |

## Construction Materials - Materiales de construción

Building supply companies carry an ever-growing number of items. When a Hispanic sub-contractor sends an employee to your store who doesn't speak English, how can you avoid tie-ups at the cash register? Do you have a strategy prepared to help you if the customer comes into the store with a list of needed materials written *en español?* Refer to the following vocabulary. Start by greeting your customer, and telling him or her that you speak a little Spanish. Then ask the customer what he needs. To help you get started, review the vocabulary in page20. Chances are even your English-speaking customers will hold you in high regard when they see your new customer service plan *en acción*.

**¿Qué necesita, Señor?**            **(kay nay-say-SEE-ta, sen-YOUR)**

| English | Español | Guide |
|---------|---------|-------|
| ½" 3-ply | Madera laminada de tres capas<br><br>un medio de pulgada | ma-**DAY**-rah la-me-**NA**-da day trays **CA**-pas<br><br>un **MAY**-d-oh day pool-**GA**-da |
| ½" 4-ply | Madera laminada de cuatro capas –<br><br>un medio de pulgada | ma-**DAY**-rah la-me-**NA**-da day coo-**AH**-trow **CA**-pas<br><br>un **MAY**-d-oh day pool-**GA**-da |
| ½" PT | Un medio –<br><br>Tratado de presión | un **MAY**-d-oh<br><br>tra-**TA**-doe day pray-see-**ON** |
| ¾" PT | Tres cuartos –<br><br>Tratado de presión | trays coo-**ARE**-toes<br><br>tra-**TA**-doe day pray-see-**ON** |
| 2x4 | Dos por cuatro | dose pour coo-**AH**-trow |
| 2x6 | Dos por seis | dose pour **SAY**-ees |
| 2x8 | Dos por ocho | dose pour **OH**-cho |
| Particle board | Tabla de partículo<br>*or*<br>Madera prensada | **TA**-blah day par-**T**-coo-low ma-**DAY**-rah pren-**SA**-da |

| English | Español | Guide |
|---|---|---|
| Asphalt shingles | Ripias de asfalto<br>*or*<br>Tejamaní de asfalto | **REE**-p-ahs day<br>as-**FALL**-toe<br>tay-ha-ma-**KNEE** day<br>as-**FALL**-toe |
| Attic fan | Ventilador de ático | ven-t-la-**DOOR** day<br>**AH**-t-co |
| Bag | Bolsa | **BOWL**-sa |
| Ball peen hammer | Martillo de bola | mar-**TEE**-yo day<br>**BOW**-la |
| Bathroom fan | Ventilador de baño | ven-t-la-**DOOR** day<br>**BAHN**-yo |
| Bill | Factura | fac-**TOO**-rah |
| Blade (circular saw)<br>Jigsaw Blade | Disco<br>Hoja | **DEES**-co<br>**OH**-ja |
| Board | Tabla | **TA**-blah |
| Board (gypsum) | Muro de yeso<br>Tablaroca<br>Chirok<br>Sheetrock<br>Drywall | **MOO**-row day **YEA**-so<br>**TA**-blah-**ROW**-ka<br>**CHEE**-rock<br>Sheetrock<br>Drywall |
| Bolt | Perno | **PEAR**-no |
| Box | Caja | **CA**-ha |
| Broad knife | Espátula ancha | ace-**PA**-too-la<br>**AHN**-cha |
| Brush | Cepillo | say-**P**-yo |
| Cabinet grade | Grado de gabinete | **GRA**-doe day<br>ga-b-**NET**-tay |
| Calk line | Línea de tiza | **LEE**-nay-ah day **T**-sa |
| Caulk gun | Pistola de sellador | peas-**TOE**-la day<br>say-ya-**DOOR** |
| Cedar | Cedro | **SAY**-drow |
| Ceiling far | Ventilador de<br>techo | ven-t-la-**DOOR** day<br>**TAY**-cho |
| Chalk string | Cordel entizado | core-**DELL** n-t-**SA**-doe |
| Cherry | Cerezo | say-**RAY**-so |
| Concrete | Concreto | con-**CRAY**-toe |
| Conduit (cable) | Conducto de cables | con-**DUKE**-toe day<br>**CA**-blays |

| English | Español | Guide |
|---|---|---|
| Conduit (pipe) | Conducto | con-**DUKE**-toe |
| | Tubo | **TOO**-bow |
| Contractor | Contratista | con-tra-**TEES**-ta |
| Corrugated metal | Metal corrugado | may-**TAL** |
| | | core-roo-**GA**-doe |
| Counter top | Mostrador | mos-**TRA**-door |
| Crown molding | Cornisa | corn-**KNEE**-sa |
| Depth | Profundidad | pro-foon-d-**DAD** |
| Dimensional lumber | Barrote dimensional | ba-**ROW**-tay |
| | | d-men-see-on-**NAL** |
| Dowel | Taco | **TA**-co |
| | Clavija | cla-**V**-ha |
| Downspout | Bajada de aguas | ba-**HA**-da day |
| | | **AH**-goo-ahs |
| Drywall | Muro de yeso | **MOO**-row day **YEA**-so |
| | *or* | |
| | Tablaroca | **TA**-blah-**ROW**-ka |
| | *or* | |
| | Chirok | **CHEE**-rock |
| | *or* | |
| | Sheetrock | Sheetrock |
| | *or* | |
| | Drywall | Drywall |
| Drywall screws | Tornillos de tablaroca | tore-**KNEE**-yos day **TA**-blah-**ROW**-ka |
| Drywall, fiberglass | Muro de fibra de vidrio | **MOO**-row day **FEE**-bra day **VEED**-ree-oh |
| Edge | Borde | **BORE**-day |
| Edge strips | Tira de borde | T-rah day **BORE**-day |
| Electric cord | Extensión eléctrica | x-ten-see-**ON** a-**LEC**-tree-ca |
| Epoxy putty | Masilla epóxica | ma-**SEE**-ya a-**POX**-see-ca |
| Exterior | Exterior | x-ter-ree-**OR** |
| Face mask | Mascarilla protectora | mas-ca-**REE**-ya pro-tec-**TOR**-rah |
| Fertilizer | Fertilzante | fer-teal-**SAHN**-tay |

| English | Español | Guide |
|---------|---------|-------|
| Finish (wood) | Acabado | ah-ca-**BA**-doe |
| Finish (rough) | Acabado ordinario | ah-ca-**BA**-doe<br>or-d-**NAR**-ree-oh |
| Finish – smooth | Acabado liso | ah-ca-**BA**-doe **LEE**-so |
| Finish grade | Calidad del terminado<br><br>*or*<br>Calidad del acabado<br><br>*or*<br>Acabado final | ca-lee-**DAD** dell<br>ter-me-**NA**-doe<br><br>ca-lee-**DAD** dell<br>ah-ca-**BA**-doe<br><br>ah-ca-**BA**-doe<br>fee-**NAL** |
| Fire rated plywood | Madera laminada<br>tasado para incendios | ma-**DAY**-rah<br>la-me-**NA**-da ta-**SA**-doe<br>**PA**-ra een-**SEND**-e-ohs |
| Fire retardant | Retardador de incendios | ray-tar-da-**DOOR** day<br>een-**SEND**-e-ohs |
| Fluorescent light | Luz fluorescente | loose<br>flu-or-es-**SENT**-tay |
| Foot | Pie | p-**A** |
| Galvanized | Galvanizado | gal-va-knee-**SA**-doe |
| Gloves | Guantes | goo-**AHN**-tays |
| Glue gun | Pistola de pegamento | peas-**TOE**-la day<br>pay-ga-**MEN**-toe |
| Golden oak | Roble dorado | **ROBE**-lay<br>door-**RA**-doe |
| Grain | Veta | **VAY**-ta |
| Granite | Granito | grah-**KNEE**-toe |
| Grout | Lechada<br>*or*<br>Cemento decorativo | lay-**CHA**-da<br><br>say-**MEN**-toe<br>day-core-rah-**TEEV**-oh |
| Gypsum | Yeso | **YEA**-so |
| Half | Medio | **MAY**-d-oh |
| Hard wood | Madera dura | ma-**DAY**-rah **DO**-rah |
| Hardware | Cerrajería | say-rah-hey-**REE**-ah |
| Hedge trimmer | Recortador de arbustos | ray-core-ta-**DOOR** day<br>are-**BOO**-stows |

| English | Español | Guide |
|---|---|---|
| Height | Altura | Al-**TOO**-rah |
| HVAC | Calefacción-ventilación y aire acondicionado | cal-lay-fax-see-**ON** ven-t-la-see-**ON** e **EYE**-ray ah-con-d-see-oh-**NA**-doe |
| Inch | Pulgada | Pool-**GA**-da |
| Insulating material | Material aislante | ma-tay-ree-**AL** ice-**LAHN**-tay |
| Insulation | Aislante | ice-**LAHN**-tay |
| Interior | Interior | een-ter-ree-**OR** |
| Iron | Hierro | e-**A**-row |
| Joiner | Carpintero | Car-peen-**TAY**-row |
| Joint compound | Masa de yeso | **MA**-sa day **YEA**-so |
| Joist | Vigueta | v-**GET**-ah |
| Latex | Látex | **LA**-tex |
| Length | Largo | **LAR**-go |
| Light | Luz | loose |
| Light bulb | Foco | **FO**-co |
| Lime | Cal | cal |
| Linoleum | Linóleo | Lee-**NO**-lay-oh |
| Lubricant | Lubricante | Loo-bree-**CAN**-tay |
| Lumber | Madera de construcción | Ma-**DAY**-rah day con-strook-see-**ON** |
| Mahogany | Caoba | Ca-**OH**-ba |
| Mallet | Mazo | **MA**-so |
| Maple | Arce | **ARE**-say |
| Marble | Mármol | **MAR**-mol |
| Mastic | Mastique | mass-**T**-kay |
| Metal sheeting | Lámina de metal | **LA**-me-na day **MAY**-tal |
| Mildew | Moho | **MO**-ho |
| Nail gun | Pistola de clavos | peas-**TOE**-la day **CLA**-vos |
| | Pistola | peas-**TOE**-la |
| Paint | Pintura | peen-**TOO**-rah |
| Paint brush | Brocha | **BRO**-cha |
| Paint roller | Rodillo | row-**D**-yo |

| English | Español | Guide |
|---|---|---|
| Paint tray | Cacerola de pintura | ca-say-**ROLL**-ah day peen-**TOO**-rah |
| Paneling | Paneles | pa-**NELL**-ace |
| Paste | Pegamento | pay-ga-**MEN**-toe |
| Patch | Parche | **PAR**-chay |
| Pine | Pino | **P**-no |
| Pipe | Tubo | **TO**-bow |
| Plank | Tablón | Ta-**BLAWN** |
| Plaster | Yeso | **YEA**-so |
| Plywood | Madera laminada | ma-**DAY**-rah la-me-**NA**-da |
|  | Madera prensada | ma-**DAY**-rah pren-**SA**-da |
| Polyethylene | Polietileno | po-lee-a-t-**LAY**-no |
| Porch | Pórtico | **POUR**-t-co |
| Pre-cast | Precolado | pray-co-**LA**-doe |
| Prefabricated | Prefabricado | pray-fah-bree-**CA**-doe |
| Primer | Base | **BA**-say |
| Propane | Propano | pro-**PA**-no |
| Putty | Masilla | ma-**SEE**-ya |
|  | Mástique | **MASS**-t-kay |
| Putty knife | Espátula angosta | ace-**PA**-too-la an-**GHOST**-ta |
| PVC | Pe Ve Ce | pay vay say |
| Reinforced | Reforzado | ray-four-**SA**-doe |
| Resin | Resina | ray-**SEE**-na |
| Roll | Rollo | **ROW**-yo |
| Roofing felt | Tela asfáltica | **TAY**-la ahs-**FALL**-t-ca |
| Roofing hammer | Martillo de teja | mar-**T**-yo day **TAY**-ha |
| Rough | Áspero | **AHS**-pay-row |
| Round | Redondo | ray-**DON**-doe |
| Sand | Arena | ah-**RAY**-na |
| Sander | Lijadora | lee-ha-**DOOR**-rah |
| Saw blade | Hoja de sierra | **OH**-ha day see-**AIR**-rah |

| English | Español | Guide |
|---------|---------|-------|
| Sawn timber | Madera aserradas | ma-**DAY**-rah ah-say-**RAH**-das |
| Screw | Tornillo | Tore-**KNEE**-yo |
| Screw gun | Atornillador eléctrico | ah-tore-lee-na-**DOOR** a-**LEC**-tree-co |
| Screwdriver | Destornillador | des-tore-knee-ya-**DOOR** |
| Screwdriver, flat | Destornillador plano | des-tore-knee-ya-**DOOR PLA**-no |
| Screwdriver, Phillips | Destornillador de cruz | des-tore-knee-ya-**DOOR** day cruise |
| Sheeting | Lámina | **LA**-mee-na |
| Shingle | Ripia | **REE**-p-ah |
| Shingling hammer | Martillo para tejamanil | mar-**T**-yo **PA**-rah tay-ha-ma-**KNEEL** |
| Silicone | Silicón | see-lee-**CONE** |
| Silicone sealant | Sellador de silicón | say-ya-**DOOR** day see-lee-**CONE** |
| Skirting board | Zoclo | **SO**-clo |
| Slab | Losa | **LOW**-sa |
| Slate | Pizarra | p-**SA**-rah |
| Sledgehammer | Marro | **MA**-row |
| Smooth | Liso | **LEE**-so |
| Soldering gun | Cautín | cow-**TEEN** |
| Spackle | Junta de cemento | **WHOON**-ta day say-**MEN**-toe |
| Spray paint gun | Pistola de pintar | peas-**TOE**-la day peen-**TAR** |
| Stain | Tinta | **TEEN**-ta |
| Stainless steel | Acero inoxidable | ah-**SAY**-row een-ox-see-**DA**-blay |
| Staple | Grapa | **GRA**-pa |
| Staple gun | Pistola de engrapar | peas-**TE**-la day een-grah-**PAR** |
| Staple puller | Desengrapadora | des-een-gra-pa-**DOOR**-ah |
| Steel | Acero | ah-**SAY**-row |

| English | Español | Guide |
| --- | --- | --- |
| Stud | Soporte | so-**POUR**-tay |
| Supplier | Proveedor | pro-vay-a-**DOOR** |
| Torch (acetylene) | Antorcha de acetileno | an-**TORE**-cha day ah-say-t-**LAY**-no |
| Torch (propane) | Antorcha de propano | an-**TORE**-cha day pro-**PA**-no |
| Varnish | Barniz | bar-**NIECE** |
| Veneer | Chapado | cha-**PA**-doe |
| Wall board | Hojas de fibra prensada<br><br>Cartón de yeso | **OH**-has day **FEE**-bra pren-**SA**-da<br>car-**TONE** day **YEA**-so |
| Walnut | Nogal | no-**GAHL** |
| Waterproof | Impermeable | em-pear-may-**AH**-blay |
| Waterproofing substance | Impermeabilizante | em-pear-may-ah-b-lee-**SAN**-tay |
| Welding mask | Careta para soldar | ca-**RAY**-ta **PA**-rah sol-**DAR** |
| Width | De ancha | day **AHN**-cha |
| Wire brush | Cepillo de alambre | say-**P**-yo day ah-**LAMB**-bray |
| Wood flooring | Piso de madera | **P**-so day ma-**DAY**-rah |
| Wood putty | Masilla de madera | ma-**SEE**-ya day ma-**DAY**-rah |
| Wood screw | Tornillo para madera | tore-**KNEE**-yo **PA**-rah ma-**DAY**-rah |
| Work bench | Banco de trabajo | **BAHN**-co day tra-**BA**-jo |

## Masonry

| English | Español | Guide |
| --- | --- | --- |
| ¾ header | Ladrillo de tres cuartos de pared | la-**DREE**-yo day trays coo-**ARE**-toes day pa-**RED** |
| Arch | Arco | **ARE**-co |

| English | Español | Guide |
|---|---|---|
| Arch brick | Ladrillo de arco | la-**DREE**-yo day **ARE**-co |
| Bag | Bolsa | **BOWL**-sa |
| Brace | Riostra | ree-**OH**-stra |
| Brick | Ladrillo | la-**DREE**-yo |
| Brick clamp | Corchete para ladrillos | core-**CHAY**-tay **PA**-rah la-**DREE**-yos |
| Brick hammer | Martillo de enladrillador | Mar-**T**-yo day n-la-dree-la-**DOOR** |
| Brick laid on edge | Ladrillos a canto | la-**DREE**-yos ah **CAN**-toe |
| Brick laid on end | Ladrillos de testa | la-**DREE**-yos day **TES**-ta |
| Bricklayer | Albañil | al-ban-**YEEL** |
| Brick up | Enladrillar | n-la-dree-**YAR** |
| Brick wall | Muro de ladrillos | **MOO**-row day la-**DREE**-yos |
| Bucket | Cubo | **COO**-bow |
| Cell | Célula | **SAY**-loo-la |
| Concrete | Concreto | con-**CRAY**-toe |
| Concrete brick | Ladrillo de concreto | la-**DREE**-yo day con-**CRAY**-toe |
| Cover | Tapa | **TA**-pa |
| Course | Capa | **CA**-pa |
| Edger | Borde | **BORE**-day |
| Face brick | Ladrillo de fachada | la-**DREE**-yo day fa-**CHA**-da |
| Fire brick | Ladrillo de fuego | la-**DREE**-yo day foo-**A**-go |
| Float | Flotador | flow-ta-**DOOR** |
| Foot | Pie | p-**A** |
| Grout | Lechada de cemento | Lay-**CHA**-da day say-**MEN**-toe |
| Header | Ladrillo a tizón | la-**DREE**-yo ah t-**SEWN** |
| Hod | Cuezo | coo-**WAY**-so |
| Hollow brick | Ladrillo alivianado | la-**DREE**-yo ah-lee-v-an-**AH**-doe |

| English | Español | Guide |
|---|---|---|
| Inch | Pulgada | pull-**GA**-da |
| Insulating brick | Ladrillo aislador | la-**DREE**-yo ice-la-**DOOR** |
| Jamb brick | Ladrillo de jamba | la-**DREE**-yo day **HAM**-ba |
| Jointer | Escarbador de juntas | es-car-ba-**DOOR** day **WHOON**-tas |
| Level | Nivel | knee-**VELL** |
| Mortar | Mortero | more-**TAY**-row |
| Mortar mixer | Mezclador de mortero | Mace-cla-**DOOR** day more-**TAY**-row |
| Mud | Lodo | **LO**-doe |
| Neck brick | Ladrillo de cuello | la-**DREE**-yo day coo-**WAY**-yo |
| Pavement | Enladrillado | n-la-dree-**LA**-doe |
| Paver | Pavimento | pa-v-**MEN**-toe |
| Plumb line | Plomada | plow-**MA**-da |
| Precast | Hormigón en bloques | or-me-**GONE** in **BLOCK**-ace |
| Rake | Rastrillo | ras-**TREE**-yo |
| Rebar | Varilla | var-**REE**-ya |
| Reinforce | Reforzado | ray-for-**SA**-doe |
| Row / line | Hilera | e-**LAIR**-ah |
| Rowlock | Ladrillos a sardinel | la-**DREE**-yos ah sar-d-**NELL** |
| Sand | Arena | ah-**RAY**-na |
| Scaffold | Andamio | an-da-**ME**-oh |
| Scrapper | Raspador | rasp-ah-**DOOR** |
| Shovel | Pala | **PA**-la |
| Sidewalk | Banqueta | ban-**KAY**-ta |
| Sill | Umbral | oom-**BRAL** |
| Smooth brick | Ladrillo liso | la-**DREE**-yo **LEE**-so |
| Soldier course | Hilera de ladrillos colocados de cabeza | e-**LAIR**-rah day la-**DREE**-yos co-low-**CA**-dose day ca-**BAY**-sa |
| Stamped concrete | Concreto estampado | con-**CRAY**-toe es-stam-**PA**-doe |

| English | Español | Guide |
|---|---|---|
| Stone | Piedra | p-**A**-dra |
| Stretcher | Ladrillo al hilo | la-**DREE**-yo al –**E**-low |
| | Ladrillo de soga | la-**DREE**-yo day **SO**-ga |
| Tile cutters | Cortador de loza | core-ta-**DOOR** day **LOW**-sa |
| Tiler | Tejador | tay-ha-**DOOR** |
| Trowel | Paleta | pa-**LAY**-ta |
| Wheelbarrow | Carretilla | car-ray-**T**-ya |
| Wythe | Media citara | may-**D**-ah see-**TAR**-ah |

## Masonry Verbs

| English | Español | Guide |
|---|---|---|
| To… | | |
| Caulk | Calafatear | ca-la-fa-tay-**ARE** |
| Clean | Limpiar | leem-p-**ARE** |
| Cut | Cortar | core-**TAR** |
| Drill | Perforar | pear-for-**ARE** |
| Drive (a car) | Manejar | man-nay-**HAR** |
| Drive (a nail) | Clavar | cla-**VAR** |
| Grout | Inyectar lechada | en-yec-**TAR** lay-**CHA**-da |
| Lay | Enladrillar | n-la-dree-**YAR** |
| Mix | Mezclar | mess-**CLAR** |
| Pour | Colar | co-**LAR** |
| Scrape | Raspar | rahs-**PAR** |
| Set up (dry) | Secar | say-**CAR** |
| Stack | Apilar | ah-p-**LAR** |
| Stop | Parar | pa-**RAR** |
| Tie | Ligar | lee-**GAR** |
| Tile floors | Losar | low-**SAR** |

# Important People – Personas Importantes

| English | Español | Guide |
|---|---|---|
| Builder | Constructor | con-strewk-**TOR** |
| Crew leader | Líder de equipo | **LEE**-dare day a-**KEY**-po |
| Fork lift operator | Operario de carretilla elevadora | oh-pear-**RAR**-ree-oh day car-ray-**TEE**-ya a-lay-va-**DOOR**-ah |
| Gantry supervisor | Supervisor de pórtico | sue-pear-vee-**SOAR** day **POUR**-tee-co |
| Maintenance | Mantenimiento | mahn-te-knee-me-**N**-toe |
| Maintenance supervisor | Supervisor de mantenimiento | sue-pear-vee-**SOAR** day mahn-te-knee-me-**N**-toe |
| Manager Boss | Gerente Jefe | hair-**RENT**-tay **HEF**-ay |
| Probationary associate | Asociado a prueba | ah-so-see-**AH**-doe ah pru-**A**-baa |
| Receptionist | Recepcionista | ray-cep-see-o-**NEES**-ta |
| Saw catchers | Receptores de sierra | ray-cep-**TOR**-aces day see-**AIR**-ra |
| Saw supervisor | Supervisor de sierra | Sue-pear-vee-**SOAR** day see-**AIR**-ra |
| Sawyer | Aserradores | Ah-ser-ra-**DOOR**-rays |
| Secretary | Secretaria/Secretario | Sec-ray-**TAR**-ree-ah Sec-ray-**TAR**-ree-oh |
| Stacker | Apilador | Ah-pee-la-**DOOR** |
| Yard supervisor | Supervisor del patio | Sue-pear-v-**SOAR** del **PA**-tee-oh |

# Important Machines – Máquinas Importantes

| English | Español | Guide |
|---|---|---|
| Fire Suppression System | Sistemas de supresión de incendios | sees-**TAY**-mas day sue-pray-see-**ON** day een-**SEND**-dee-ohs |
| Fork Lift | Caretilla elevadora | ca-ray-**TEE**-ya a-lay-va-**DOOR**-ra |
| Framing Table | Mesa de preparación de los marcos | **MAY**-sa day pray-pa-ra-see-**ON** day los **MAR**-cos |
| Gantry Press | Prensa de pórtico | **PREN**-sa day **POUR**-tee-co |
| Nail Gun | Pistolas de clavar | pees-**TOE**-las day cla-**VAR** |
| Pinch Press | Prensa de rodillo a presión | **PREN**-sa day row-**DEE**-yo ah pray-see-**ON** |
| Saw | Sierra | see-**AY**-ra |
| Squaring Table | Mesa de Escuadrado | **MAY**-sa day es-coo-**AH**-dra-doe |

# Safety Is Number One - *Seguridad Es Número Uno*

Safety is a major concern at construction sites. The fatality rate of Hispanics in construction is three times that of other workers. It's important to realize that some of your Latino employees will be quite unfamiliar with some of the tools and safety procedures required for the work you're doing. In some Latin American countries safety rules are almost nonexistent!

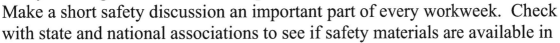

Making a commitment to training and good communications will help you prevent many accidents. That's just good business. Talk about safety on a regular basis. Ask for opinions.

Make a short safety discussion an important part of every workweek. Check with state and national associations to see if safety materials are available in

Spanish. You're going to be pleasantly surprised! OSHA is a particularly good resource. At www.osha.gov you will find a variety of dictionaries with construction terms in addition to health and safety materials translated into Spanish. Also, the key phrases and the vocabulary below will help you.

| English | Español | Guide |
|---|---|---|
| Hard hat | Casco | **KAS**-co |
| Danger! | ¡Peligro! | pay-**LEE**-grow |
| Accident | Accidente | ax-see-**DENT**-tay |
| Anchor point | Punto de anclaje | **POON**-toe day **AN**-cla-hay |
| Barricade | Barricada | bar-ree-**KA**-da |
| Be careful. | Tenga cuidado. | **TEN**-gah kwee-**DA**-doe |
| Bruised | Golpeadas | gol-pay-**AH**-das |
| Burns | Quemadas | kay-**MA**-dahs |
| Cleanliness | Limpieza | limp-p-**ACE**-ah |
| Crane boom | Brazo de grúas | **BRA**-so day **GREW**-ahs |
| Defect | Defecto | day-**FEC**-toe |
| Electrocution | Electrocución | a-lec-tro-cue-see-**ON** |
| Excavation | Excavación | x-ka-vah-see-**ON** |
| Falls | Caídas | ca-**EE**-das |
| Fire | Fuego | foo-**A**-go |
| Fire extinguisher | Extinguidor de fuego | x-ting-gee-**DOR** day foo-**A**-go |
| First aid | Primeros auxilios | pre-**MAY**-rows aux-**E**-lee-ohs |
| Fractures | Fracturas | frac-**TO**-ras |
| Front End loader | Cargadora de ataque frontal | car-gah-**DOOR**-ah day ah-**TACK**-ay fron-**TAL** |
| Gasoline | Gasolina | gas-oh-**LEAN**-ah |
| Guardrail | Barandillas | ba-ran-**DEE**-yas |
| Harness | Arnés | are-**NES** |
| Heat exhaustion | Agotamiento de calor | ah-go-ta-me-N-toe day ca-**LORE** |
| High top safety boots | Botas de seguridad bien ajustadas | **BOW**-tas day say-goo-ree-**DAD** b-N ah-whos-**TAH**-dahs |

94

| English | Español | Guide |
|---|---|---|
| High voltage | Alto voltaje | **AL**-toe vowl-**TA**-hey |
| Hoisting | Levantamiento | lay-van-ta-me-**N**-toe |
| Maintenance | Mantenimiento | man-ten-knee-me-**N**-toe |
| No smoking. | No fumar | no foo-**MAR** |
| Outrigger | Batanga | ba-**TANG**-ga |
| Platform | Plataforma | pla-ta-**FOR**-ma |
| Protection | Protección | pro-teck-see-**ON** |
| Pulling nails | Sacando clavos | sa-**CAN**-doe **CLA**-vows |
| Rigging | Sujeción | soo-heck-see-**ON** |
| Safety belt | Cinturón de seguridad | seen-to-**RON** day say-goo-ree-**DAD** |
| Safety glasses | Anteojos de seguridad | anti-**OH**-hos day say-goo-ree-**DAD** |
| | Gafas de protección | **GA**-fas day pro-tec-see-**ON** |
| Scaffold | Andamio | an-da-**ME**-oh |
| Scraped | Raspadas | ras-**PA**-das |
| Shirt | Camisa | ca-**ME**-sa |
| Shoring | Apuntalamiento | ah-poon-ta-la-me-**N**-toe |
| Strained | Distendidas | des-ten-**DEE**-das |
| Trench | Zanjas | **SAN**-has |
| Wire rope | Cable de acero | **KA**-blay day ah-**SER**-row |

## Lock Out – Tag Out

Lock out–tag out vocabulary is essential to a variety of professions, especially those which involve large dangerous machines. To learn these words and phrases in Spanish, go through the list and highlight the terms you use most often. Look at the pronunciation guide and sound the words out. Always remember, in a SpeakEasy pronunciation guide, the bold capital letters indicate the part of the word that receives vocal emphasis.

| English | Español | Guide |
|---|---|---|
| Lockout Tagout | Cierre y Etiquetado | see-**EH**-ray e eh-t-kay-**TA**-doe |
| Do not operate | No operar | no oh-pear-**RAR** |
| Do not start | No arrancar | no ah-rahn-**CAR** |
| Do not use | No usar | no oo-**SAR** |
| Jammed | Atascado | ah-tahs-**CA**-doe |
| Manually | Manualmente | man-oo-ahl-**MEN**-tay |
| Moving parts | Partes móviles | **PAR**-tays **MO**-v-lace |
| Never ignore tags | Nunca ignore una etiqueta | **NOON**-ca eg-**NOR**-ay **OO**-na eh-t-**KAY**-ta |
| Normal operations | Operaciones normales | oh-pear-ra-see-**ON**-ace nor-**MAL**-lace |
| Notify | Notificar | no-t-fee-**CAR** |
| Off/shut down | Apagado | ah-pa-**GA**-doe |
| On | Prendido | pren-**D**-doe |
| One key per lock | Una llave por candado | **OO**-na **YA**-vay pour can-**DA**-doe |
| Plug in | Enchufar | n-chew-**FAR** |
| Procedure for shut down | Procedimiento de cierre | pro-said-d-me-**N**-toe day see-**EH**-ray |
| Remove a lock | Quitar un candado | key-**TAR** oon can-**DA**-doe |
| Remove a tag | Quitar una etiqueta | key-**TAR OO**-na eh-t-**KAY**-ta |
| Safety | Seguridad | say-goo-ree-**DAD** |
| Safety device | Aditamento de seguridad | ah-d-ta-**MEN**-toe day say-goo-ree-**DAD** |
| Maintenance work | Trabajo de servicio | tra-**BA**-jo day ser-**V**-see-oh |

## Please, Call a Doctor! - ¡Favor de llamar un doctor!

Construction is a dangerous profession, and on-the-job accidents can happen even in the safest workplaces. Quick reaction time and good communication skills are critical in the event of an emergency. Learning these parts of the body will help you- and could save a life!

| English | Español | Guide |
|---------|---------|-------|
| Ankle | Tobillo | toe-**BEE**-yo |
| Arm | Brazo | **BRA**-so |
| Back | Espalda | es-**PALL**-doe |
| Body | Cuerpo | coo-**AIR**-poe |
| Brain | Cerebro | say-**RAY**-bro |
| Chest | Pecho | **PAY**-cho |
| Chin | Barbilla | bar-**BEE**-ya |
| Ear | Oreja | oh-**RAY**-ha |
| Eye | Ojo | **OH**-ho |
| Face | Cara | **CA**-ra |
| Finger | Dedo | **DAY**-do |
| Foot | Pie | p-**A** |
| Hand | Mano | **MA**-no |
| Head | Cabeza | ca-**BAY**-sa |
| Heart | Corazón | core-ra-**SEWN** |
| Knee | Rodilla | row-**DEE**-ya |
| Leg | Pierna | p-**YAIR**-na |
| Mouth | Boca | **BOW**-ca |
| Nail | Uña | **OON**-ya |
| Neck | Cuello | coo-**A**-yo |
| Nose | Nariz | **NA**-reece |
| Skin | Piel | p-**L** |
| Shoulder | Hombro | **ON**-bro |
| Spine | Espina | es-**PEE**-na |
| Stomach | Estómago | es-**TOE**-ma-go |
| Throat | Garganta | gar-**GAN**-ta |
| Toe | Dedo del pie | **DAY**-doe del **PEE**-ya |
| Tooth | Diente | d-**N**-tay |
| Wrist | Muñeca | moon-**YAY**-ca |

## Other Common Problems – Otros Problemas Comunes

Perhaps you or your employees have something more complicated than a simple ache or pain. Maybe there's a problem that requires further medical advice. Here is a list of symptoms and conditions that you could encounter. Some of these could cause employee absences and in some cases workmen's compensation claims.

| English | Español | Guide |
|---|---|---|
| Abscess | Absceso | ab-**SAY**-so |
| Blister | Ampolla | am-**PO**-ya |
| Broken bone | Hueso roto | who-**AY**-so **ROW**-toe |
| Bruise | Contusión | con-too-see-**ON** |
| Bump | Hinchazón | eem-cha-**SEWN** |
| Burn | Quemadura | kay-ma-**DO**-ra |
| Chills | Escalofrío | es-ca-low-**FREE**-oh |
| Cough | Tos | toes |
| Cramps | Calambre | ca-**LAMB**-bray |
| Diarrhea | Diarrea | dee-ah-**RAY**-ah |
| Fever | Fiebre | fee-**A**-bray |
| Indigestion | Indigestión | een-dee-hes-tee-**ON** |
| Lump | Bulto | **BOOL**-toe |
| Migraine | Jaqueca | ja-**KAY**-ca |
| Pain | Dolor | doe-**LORE** |
| Rash | Erupción | a-roop-see-**ON** |
| Sprain | Torcedura | tor-say-**DO**-ra |
| Swelling | Inflamación | een-fla-ma-see-**ON** |
| Wound | Herido | a-**REE**-doe |

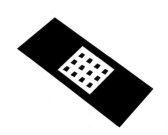

## Other Phrases to Describe an Illness

|  |  |
|---|---|
| Yo toso. | I'm coughing. |
| Yo no puedo dormir. | I can't sleep. |
| Yo estornudo. | I'm sneezing. |
| Yo estoy agotado (a). | I'm exhausted. |
| Yo tengo náusea. | I'm nauseous. |
| Me duele todo el cuerpo. | I hurt everywhere. |
| Yo estoy sangrando. | I'm bleeding. |
| Me siento mal. | I feel bad. |

# One for the Road: Phrases to Use Any Time

Obviously, conversation is made up of more than just lists of words. It will take practice and determination for you to achieve free-flowing conversation in a language that's new to you. Learning Spanish is a slow and steady process for adults. It could take several months before you begin to "think" in Spanish, so don't expect to achieve native speaker speed over night! There will be times when you feel like you can't remember anything you've studied. That's natural. It happens to everyone. Try not to be discouraged. The rewards you'll receive from learning to speak Spanish are far greater than a little bit of frustration. If you keep working, it won't be long before you'll have a break-through. Learning Spanish is a lot like eating a great steak. You don't want to rush it. Cut each bite of your Spanish, chew it over carefully and savor each morsel. Moving along at a slower pace will help you retain what you learn longer.

Spanish is a language that has loads of zest and flair. It is punctuated with single words and short phrases that can really express a lot of sentiment. The next time you have an opportunity to observe native speakers, listen carefully. You may hear them switch from English to Spanish, depending on what they are saying. And, you might hear them use any of the "one-liners" listed below. Phrases like these add spice to your conversation. Use the following list to help you take your conversational skills to the next level.

| English | Español | Guide |
|---------|---------|-------|
| Are you sure? | ¿Está seguro? (a) | es-**TA** say-**GOO**-row |
| Excellent! | ¡Excelente! | x-say-**LENT**-tay |
| Fantastic! | ¡Fantástico! | fan-**TA**-stee-co |
| Good idea. | Buena idea. | boo-**A**-na e-**DAY**-ah |
| Happy birthday! | ¡Feliz cumpleaños! | fay-**LEASE** coom-play-**AHN**-yos |
| Have a nice day. | Tenga un buen día. | **TEN**-ga un boo-**WAYNE DEE**-ah |
| I agree. | De acuerdo. | day ah-coo-**AIR**-doe |
| I believe so. | Creo que sí. | **CRAY**-oh kay **SEE** |
| I'm so glad. | Me alegro. | may ah-**LAY**-gro |

| English | Español | Guide |
|---|---|---|
| I'll be right back. | ¡Ahora vengo! | ah-**OR**-ah **VEIN**-go |
| I'm leaving now. | ¡Ya me voy! | ya may **VOY** |
| That's OK. | Está bien. | es-**TA** b-**N** |
| It's important. | Es importante. | es eem-pour-**TAHN**-tay |
| It's serious. | Es grave. | es **GRA**-vay |
| It's possible. | Es posible | es po-**SEE**-blay |
| Like this? | ¿Así? | ah-**SEE** |
| Maybe. | Quizás. | key-**SAHS** |
| Me, neither | Yo tampoco. | yo tam-**PO**-co |
| Me, too | Yo también. | yo tam-b-**N** |
| More or less | Más o menos. | mas oh **MAY**-nos |
| Really? | ¿De veras? | day **VER**-ahs |
| Sure | ¡Claro! | **CLA**-row |
| That depends. | Depende. | day-**PEN**-day |
| We'll see you. | Nos vemos. | nos **VAY**-mos |

## Para Practicar:

1. Name some phrases that could accompany "adiós": _____

   _____

2. Name a few words you could say when something is really great:

   _____

3. Name a few things you could say when things are going well:

   _____

4. List two phrases that you will use often:

   _____

# At the Job Site CrossWord

*Translate the English clues below into Spanish to work this crossword puzzle. The answer key is at the back of the book. ¡Buena suerte!*

Created with EclipseCrossword - www.eclipsecrossword.com

## Across

| 4. | HAMMER |
| 5. | BEAM |
| 6. | WINDOW |
| 8. | FIRE |
| 13. | CLAMP |
| 14. | STUCCO |
| 15. | KITCHEN |
| 19. | TOOL |
| 21. | DOOR |
| 22. | EMERGENCY |
| 23. | HARD HAT |
| 24. | DISHWASHER |

## Down

| 1. | MORTAR |
| 2. | NAIL |
| 3. | FREEZER |
| 7. | APPLIANCE |
| 9. | CLIPPERS |
| 10. | LADRILLO |
| 11. | TO PREPARE |
| 12. | CAN |
| 15. | BUCKET |
| 16. | DINING ROOM |
| 17. | SAW |
| 18. | WHERE |
| 20. | WOOD |

# Typing in Spanish with Your Computer
## Inserting an International Character with Shortcut Keys

When you need to type letters with accent marks or use Spanish punctuation, you will use keys that you have probably never used before!  Actually, you are *composing characters* using the **control** key.  It is located on the bottom row of keys.  You will see that it is such an important key that there is one on both sides.  It keeps the computer from moving forward one space so that the accent goes on *top* of the letter instead of *beside* it.

Always remember to hold the control key down first.  It will be the *key* to your success in word processing Spanish.  With a little practice these keys will become a normal part of your word processing skills.

**Also, if using MS Word, you may use the menu command Insert>Symbol.**

| To insert | Press |
|---|---|
| á, é, í, ó, ú, ý<br>Á, É, Í, Ó, Ú, Ý | CTRL+' (APOSTROPHE), *the letter* |
| â, ê, î, ô, û<br>Â, Ê, Î, Ô, Û | CTRL+SHIFT+^ (CARET), *the letter* |
| ã, ñ, õ<br>Ã, Ñ, Õ | CTRL+SHIFT+~ (TILDE), *the letter* |
| ä, ë, ï, ö, ü, ÿ<br>Ä, Ë, Ï, Ö, Ü, Ÿ | CTRL+SHIFT+: (COLON), *the letter* |
| ¿ | ALT+CTRL+SHIFT+? |
| ¡ | ALT+CTRL+SHIFT+! |

# Practicing What You Learned

Practice is an important part of the language learning process. The more you include practice in your daily routine, the more comfortable and fluent you will become. There is no easy way to practice. It just takes time. The key to practicing Spanish is to set realistic goals. Don't let the language learning process become overwhelming to you. Yes, there is a lot to learn, and it will take some time. But, by setting realistic goals, you have a greater chance of sticking with it. Each of us have different learning styles, so find out what works best for you and break the material down into small pieces. Some of us learn best by listening. Others need to write the words and phrases in order to visualize them. Generally the more of your senses that you involve in the learning process, the faster you will retain the information. So, focus and practice one thing at a time. It's doing the little things that will make the greatest difference in the long run. Working five minutes every day on your Spanish is *mucho* better than trying to put in an hour of practice time only once each week. Consistency in your practice is critical.

Here are some practice tips that have worked for me and others who have participated in *SpeakEasy's Survival Spanish*™ training programs over the last few years.

1. Start practicing first thing in the morning. The shower is a great place to start. Say the numbers or run through the months of the year while you wash your hair. If you practice when you start your day you are more likely to continue to practice as the day progresses.

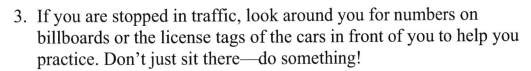

2. Use your commute time to practice. Listening to CDs, music and Spanish language radio stations will help you get the rhythm of Spanish. It will also increase your vocabulary.

3. If you are stopped in traffic, look around you for numbers on billboards or the license tags of the cars in front of you to help you practice. Don't just sit there—do something!

4. Investigate sites on the internet. Sites such as www.about.spanish.com and www.studyspanish.com are great places to practice and to learn, not to mention the fact that they are free!

5. Buy Spanish magazines or pick up Spanish newspapers that are published in your area. Many magazines like *People* have Spanish versions and almost every community in the country has a Spanish language newspaper or two. Many of them are free.

6. If there aren't any Spanish newspapers in your area, you can find a variety of publications from Latin America online. Major cities in Latin America all have newspapers that are easy to find on-line.

7. Practice as often as possible; even five minutes a day will help.

8. Don't give up! You didn't learn English overnight and you won't learn Spanish that way either. Set realistic goals and don't go too far too fast.

9. Learn five to ten words each week.

10. Practice at work with a friend.

11. Read! These books will make great additions to your library.

Baez, Francia and Chong, Nilda. *Latino Culture*. Intercultural Press, 2005

Condon, John. *Good Neighbors*. Intercultural Press, 1997

Einsohn, Marc and Steil, Gail. *The Idiot's Guide to Learning Spanish on Your Own*. Alpha Books, 1996

Hawson, Steven R. *Learn Spanish the Lazy Way*. Alpha Books, 1999.

Hogan & Associates Construction, Inc. *Construction Communication*, 1999

Kras, Eva. *Management in Two Cultures*. Intercultural Press, 1995.

Reid, Elizabeth. Spanish *Lingo for the Savvy Gringo*. In One Ear Publications, 1997

Wald, Susana. *Spanish for Dummies.* Wiley Publishing, 2000.

# Answer Key

11. Voy a trabajar.
12. Voy a terminar.
13. ¿Dónde está Ramón?
14. ¿Dónde está Carlos?
15. Soy Tim.
16. Él es Alan.
17. Ella es Amy.
18. Tengo cinco hermanas.
19. Él tiene tres hermanos.
20. Juan tiene cuatro niños.

4. The meeting is at…. Times listed run from eight until five.
   a. La reunión es a las ocho.
   b. La reunión es a las nueve.
   c. La reunión es a las diez.
   d. La reunión es a las once.
   e. La reunión es a las doce.
   f. La reunión es a la una.
   g. La reunión es a las dos.
   h. La reunión es a las tres.
   i. La reunión es a las cuatro.
   j. La reunión es a las cinco.

5. If your store opens at nine and closes at six. Your answer will be the following:
   a. La tienda abre a las nueve de la mañana.
   b. La tienda cierre a las seiz de la tarde.

6. The following work schedule is Monday through Friday from seven in the morning until 6 in the evening.
   a. Su horario es el lunes hasta el viernes de las siete de la mañana hast alas seiz en la tarde.

1. Tengo dos hijos.
2. Tengo tres hijas
3. Él tiene cuatro primos.
4. Mi esposa tiene cinco primos.
5. El nombre de mi esposa es

6. I have three uncles Tengo tres tíos.
7. Tengo seiz tías.
8. No tengo hermanos.
9. Tengo una hermana.
10. Ella no tiene niños.

**Page 51**

1. Vaya con Pablo y ayúdelo.
2. Necesito el refrigerador a la derecha.
3.  Mueve el microondas allá.
4. Hágalo ahora, por favor.
5. Quite el lavabo.
6. Apague la electricidad.
7. Apague off el agua.
8. Vaya al salón.
9. Trabaja (or Trabaje) con Esteban
10. Repara (or repare) el quemador, por favor.

**Page 63**

1. Necesita colgar cinco pies.
2. Tráigame la cola, por favor.
3. Ayuda (or Ayude) al pintor
4. ¿Dónde está la escuadra?
5. Necesito los clavos.
6. Tráigame la pistola, por favor.
7. Tráigame dos cajas de clavos.
8. Tráigame la cuerda de extención.
9. Diez pies lineales
10. Necesito quince clavijas de concreto.

# At the Job Site

*Answer Key*

Created with EclipseCrossword — www.eclipsecrossword.com

# About the Author

## Myelita Melton

Myelita Melton, founder of SpeakEasy Communications, remembers the first time she heard a "foreign" language. She knew from that moment what she wanted to do with her life. "Since I was always the kid in class that talked too much," Myelita says, "I figured it would be a good idea to learn more than one language- that way I could talk to a lot more people!" After high school, she studied in Mexico at the *Instituto de Filológica Hispánica* and completed both her BA and MA in French and Curriculum Design at Appalachian State University in Boone, NC. She has studied and speaks five languages: French, Spanish, Italian, German, and English.

"Lita's" unique career includes classroom instruction and challenging corporate experience. She has won several national awards, including a prestigious *Rockefeller* scholarship. In 1994 she was named to *Who's Who Among Outstanding Americans*. Myelita's corporate experience includes owning a television production firm, working with NBC's Spanish news division, *Canal de Noticias,* and Charlotte's PBS affiliate WTVI. In her spare time, she continues to broadcast with WDAV, a National Public Radio affiliate near Lake Norman in North Carolina where she lives.

**MEMBER**

**NATIONAL SPEAKERS ASSOCIATION**

In 1997 Myelita started SpeakEasy Communications to offer industry specific Spanish instruction in North Carolina. The company is now the nation's leader in Spanish training, offering over 30 *SpeakEasy Spanish*™ programs and publications to companies, associations, and colleges throughout the US.

Lita is also a member of the National Speaker's Association and the National Council for Continuing Education and Training. Many of her clients say she is the most high-energy, results-oriented speaker they have ever seen. As she travels the country speaking on cultural diversity issues in the workplace and languages, she has truly realized her dream of being able to speak to the world.